KU-547-222

Good Housekeeping
Cookery Club

HOT & SPICY

Janet Smith

TED SMART

A TED SMART Publication 1995

1 3 5 7 9 10 8 6 4 2

First published in the United Kingdom in 1994 by Ebury Press
Random House, 20 Vauxhall Bridge Road, London SW1V 2SA

Random House Australia (Pty) Limited
20 Alfred Street, Milsons Point, Sydney,
New South Wales 2061, Australia

Random House New Zealand Limited
18 Poland Road, Glenfield,
Auckland 10, New Zealand

Random House South Africa (Pty) Limited
PO Box 337, Bergvlei, South Africa

Random House UK Limited Reg. No. 954009

A CIP catalogue record for this book is available from the British Library.

Managing Editor: JANET ILLSLEY
Design: SARA KIDD
Special Photography: LAURIE EVANS
Food Stylist: JANET SMITH
Photographic Stylist: LESLEY RICHARDSON
Techniques Photography: KARL ADAMSON
Food Techniques Stylist: ANGELA KINGSBURY
Recipe Testing: EMMA-LEE GOW

ISBN 0 09 180548 1

Typeset in Gill Sans by Textype Typesetters, Cambridge
Colour Separations by Magnacraft, London
Printed and bound in Italy by New Interlitho Italia S.p.a., Milan

CONTENTS

COOKERY NOTES

- Both metric and imperial measures are given for the recipes. Follow either metric or imperial throughout as they are not interchangeable.
- All spoon measures are level unless otherwise stated. Sets of measuring spoons are available in both metric and imperial sizes for accurate measurement of small quantities.
- If a stage is specified under freezing instructions, the dish should be frozen at the end of that stage.
- Ovens should be preheated to the specified temperature. Grills should also be preheated. The cooking times given in the recipes assume that this has been done.
- Size 2 eggs should be used except where otherwise specified. Free-range eggs are recommended.
- Use freshly ground black pepper unless otherwise specified.
- Use fresh rather than dried herbs unless dried herbs are suggested in the recipe.

INTRODUCTION

Inspired by the wealth of exotic and mystical ingredients imported from all corners of the world, here is a collection of recipes simplified for you to recreate at home. Essential to all of them are the pungent spices and herbs that have been important in cooking throughout history.

Treat these ingredients with the respect that you would any other. Don't rely on a collection of dusty old spices that have been in the cupboard for as long as you can remember! For depth of flavour and that essential spicy 'zing', buy spices in small quantities from a shop with a fast turnover. The package should release a powerful aroma when opened.

If you have the time, buy whole spices and grind them yourself at home – this gives the best flavour by far. Use a sturdy pestle and mortar or keep a small electric coffee grinder solely for the purpose. Store both ground and whole spices in airtight containers in a cool, dark place for no more than 6 months.

As for 'hotness', that is very much a matter of personal taste. Chillies vary enormously in their strength and should always be used cautiously. Cayenne pepper, chilli powder, chilli sauce and Tabasco add heat and can also vary significantly in potency from brand to brand. Although none of the recipes in this collection is searingly hot, where these ingredients appear be guided by your personal preference.

If you prefer a very mild dish, always remove the seeds from chillies. Add half the amount of chilli or spice suggested in the recipe, taste then add more until you get the desired strength. But don't omit these ingredients altogether – even in the smallest quantities they add important background flavours. Indeed some chillies taste almost sweet and smoky and not at all hot – it is merely our perception of them that is hot.

Should you find yourself with a dish that is too hot, stir in some coconut milk, yogurt, fromage frais or cream, or serve topped with a spoonful of cooling mascarpone, yogurt or raita.

If your palate is accustomed to fiery food, be bold with your use of chillies. Search out a specialist supplier and get to know chillies in all their various forms and flavours.

Finally don't be put off by any unusual ingredients. Look to the individual recipe introductions for information or turn to pages 6-7 for an explanation and description. These ingredients add an authentic note to the recipes and in many cases a unique flavour and aroma.

Supermarkets are becoming ever more cosmopolitan in their range of goods; increasingly Thai, Indian, Mexican and Chinese ingredients are available. Some stores now have an 'ethnic' section which is an invaluable source of inspiration. Scour too the fresh herb section where you may well find packs of Indian or Thai herbs and spices.

Don't forget small specialist shops, market stalls and wholefood or healthfood shops – these often offer the best choice and need your custom.

SPECIAL INGREDIENTS

1 Dried Chillies; 2 Garlic Cloves; 3 Large Fresh Chillies; 4 Small Dried Chillies; 5 Kaffir Lime Leaves; 6 Kaffir Limes; 7 Kuchai (Garlic Chives); 8 Fennel Seeds; 9 Cloves; 10 Small Hot Fresh Chillies; 11 Moroccan Spice Mixture; 12 Lemon Grass; 13 Chilli-flavoured Oil; 14 Cardamoms; 15 Mustard Seeds; 16 Cayenne Pepper; 17 Fresh Galangal; 18 Fresh Root Ginger

GUIDE TO INGREDIENTS

CARDAMOM
Available both as tiny green pods and large black pods containing seeds, cardamom has a strong aromatic quality. Use the pods whole or for a more intense flavour take out the seeds and grind or use these whole, discarding the pods.

CAYENNE PEPPER
Made from dried red chillies. As with chillies, cayenne pepper should be used with caution as the strength varies from brand to brand.

CHILLIES
There is a wide range of fresh and dried chillies to choose from. Generally speaking the larger the chilli the milder the flavour, but there are some dramatic exceptions. The only certain way to gauge potency is by taste. So when using an unidentified batch, proceed with caution, adding a little at a time.

Whether using dried or fresh chillies, remember that their seeds and flesh can 'burn'. Wear rubber gloves for protection or at least make sure that you wash your hands thoroughly after preparation. In particular, eyes sting painfully if you happen to touch them after preparing chillies.

CINNAMON
Whole cinnamon sticks have a stronger, more intense flavour and aroma than ground cinnamon and keep their flavour for longer. However they are difficult to grind at home. Buy ground cinnamon in small quantities.

CORIANDER LEAVES
A really pungent, intensely flavoured fresh herb that you either love or hate! It looks a little like flat-leaf parsley but the leaves are more rounded and less spiky. Chop or tear into pieces or purée with spices. Fresh coriander keeps well if you buy it in a bunch with the roots attached. Stand in a jug of water, cover the leaves with a plastic bag and store in the refrigerator.

CORIANDER SEEDS
Coriander seeds taste completely different from the fresh herb. They have a fairly mild flavour and are used in many Indian, Middle Eastern and Greek dishes. Dry-roasted seeds can be ground directly onto foods.

CUMIN
A vital flavouring in curries, cumin has a strong, slightly bitter, flavour. Dry roasting gives it a milder flavour. Whole seeds keep their flavour better than ground cumin.

FENNEL SEEDS
These tiny pale green seeds lend a delicate aniseed flavour. Good with fish and vegetables.

FENUGREEK
Small hard seeds with a distinctive aroma, traditionally ground and used as a component of curry powder. Use judiciously in curries.

FIVE-SPICE POWDER
A ground spice mixture, usually containing star anise, cloves, fennel seeds, cinnamon and Chinese pepper. Blends do vary however; some contain dried orange peel. Use sparingly to give a distinctive Chinese accent.

GALANGAL
Galangal resembles fresh ginger, but is more distinctly coloured with flashes of pink. It looks dry and unappetising, but has the most wonderful flavour and aroma. It can be peeled and blended to make Thai spice pastes or used thinly sliced (without peeling) to flavour, casseroles, soups and sauces. Store in the salad drawer of the refrigerator. Dried galangal can be used instead, but it doesn't impart the same depth of flavour.

KAFFIR LIMES
Small wrinkly limes from a particular variety of lime tree. They aren't as juicy as their familiar smooth-skinned relation but they have a sweeter, more delicate flavour. Kaffir limes make an intriguing garnish. If unobtainable, use ordinary lime or lemon as a substitute.

KAFFIR LIME LEAVES

Rounded, shiny, bright green leaves with a unique flavour and scent. Use whole – like bay leaves – to flavour sauces, soups and stews, or chop or shred and use to flavour fish cakes, meat koftas, kebabs and marinades for fish and meat. Store in a plastic bag in the refrigerator.

LEMON GRASS

Long pale green stalks that are usually sold trimmed of the top dry grass-like leaves and with the tough outer leaves removed. It is the thick bottom end that has the most flavour. Bruise or crush with a rolling pin, or slice, to release maximum flavour and aroma. Store in the refrigerator or freezer.

SAFFRON

The dried stigma of the saffron crocus, saffron has a wonderful subtle flavour and aroma, and imparts a hint of yellow colour to foods it is cooked with. The whole stigmas give superior results. Powdered saffron is also available but the flavour is not as good. Although saffron is expensive a little goes a long way. A large pinch is all that is needed in most dishes.

TURMERIC

Like saffron, turmeric colours the foods that it is cooked with yellow, but that is where the similarity ends. Turmeric has a much harsher, almost earthy, flavour. Use in moderation.

SPICE AND HERB MIXTURES

Use these spice and herb mixtures as the basis for curries, soups and stews. They are easy to make. To save time you could buy jars of ready-made curry pastes, but they don't have such a powerful flavour and aroma.

THAI RED CURRY PASTE

1 small red onion or shallot
4 garlic cloves
4 cm (1½ inch) piece fresh root ginger
4 cm (1½ inch) piece fresh galangal
6-8 hot red chillies
1 lemon grass stalk
5 ml (1 tsp) shrimp paste
5 ml (1 tsp) coriander seeds
5 ml (1 tsp) salt
15 ml (1 tbsp) mild paprika
15 ml (1 tbsp) vegetable oil

1. Peel the onion or shallot and cut in half. Peel the garlic cloves. Peel the ginger and chop roughly.

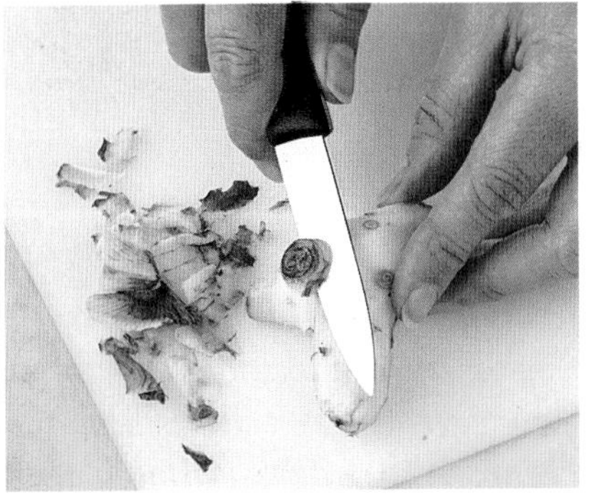

2. Using a small sharp knife, peel the galangal and trim and discard any woody or shrivelled parts. Chop roughly.

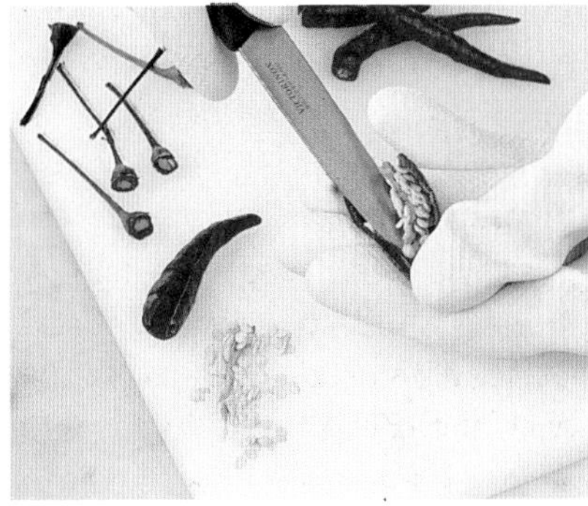

3. Remove stalks from chillies and carefully remove the seeds for a milder flavour. (Wear rubber gloves to avoid skin irritation.)

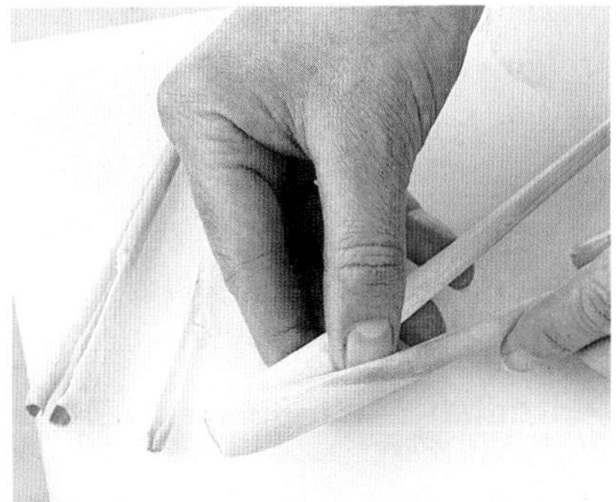

4. Peel off and discard any tough outer layers from the lemon grass. Trim the thin end. Slice the fat end.

5. Put all these ingredients in a food processor or blender and process until finely chopped.

6. Add the remaining curry paste ingredients and purée until smooth. Transfer the mixture to a screw-topped jar and store in the refrigerator for up to 3 weeks.

GREEN CURRY PASTE

8 dried green chillies
3 garlic cloves
1 onion
6 spring onions
1 lemon grass stalk
60 ml (4 tbsp) chopped fresh coriander
60 ml (4 tbsp) chopped fresh basil
5 ml (1 tsp) caraway seeds
15 ml (1 tbsp) coriander seeds
finely grated rind of 1 lime
15 ml (1 tbsp) vegetable oil

1. Carefully remove the stems and seeds from the chillies and discard (wearing rubber gloves to avoid skin irritation). Put the chillies in a small bowl, cover with boiling water and leave to soak for about 10 minutes or until softened. Drain and put in a food processor or blender.

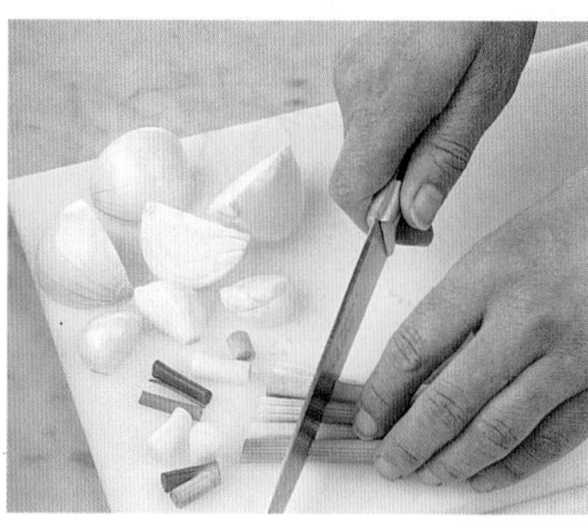

2. Peel the garlic and onion. Cut the onion into quarters. Trim and roughly chop the spring onions.

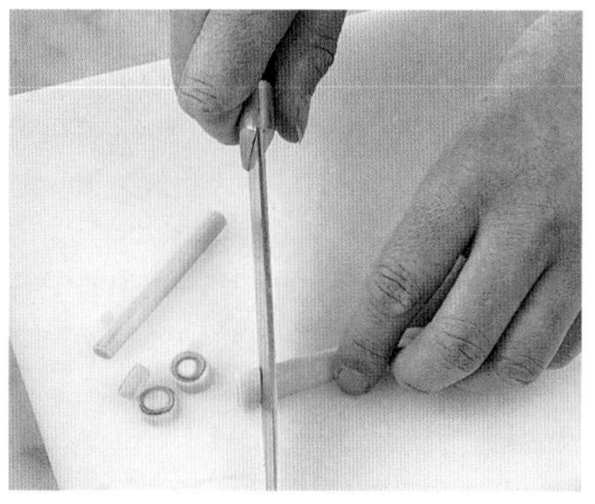

3. Peel off and discard any tough outer layers from the lemon grass. Trim the thin end. Slice the fat end.

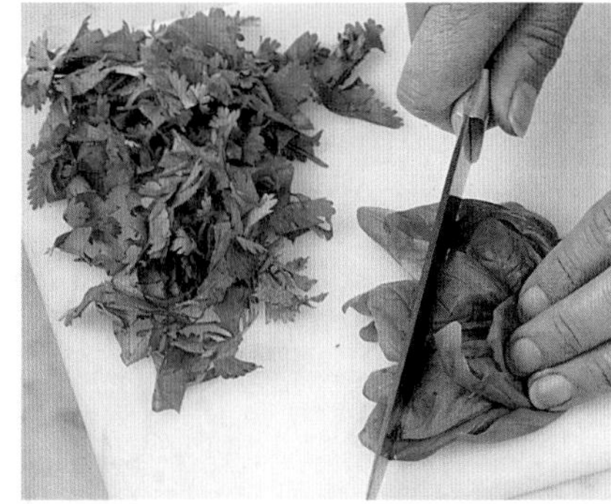

4. Roughly chop the coriander and basil.

5. Put all of the curry paste ingredients in the blender or food processor and process until smooth. Season with salt and pepper. Spoon into a screw-topped jar and store in the refrigerator for up to 3 weeks.

MOROCCAN SPICE MIXTURE

For optimum flavour make sure you use very fresh spices and grind them yourself. If they are a few months old, the flavour will not be as pungent. Use 30-45 ml (2-3 tbsp) as a marinade for meat and fish, or to flavour casseroles.

45 ml (3 tbsp) ground ginger
45 ml (3 tbsp) turmeric
45 ml (3 tbsp) coarsely ground black pepper
45 ml (3 tbsp) ground cinnamon
15 ml (1 tbsp) ground nutmeg
15 ml (1 tbsp) hot curry powder

Put all of the spices in a small bowl and mix together thoroughly. Transfer to an airtight container and use as required. Store for up to about 1 month.

CHILLI PESTO

25 g (1 oz) pine nuts
3 garlic cloves
2 hot green chillies
50 g (2 oz) fresh basil leaves
about 125 ml (4 fl oz) virgin olive oil
squeeze of lemon juice
salt and pepper

1. Toast the pine nuts under the grill or in a warm oven until golden brown. Leave to cool.

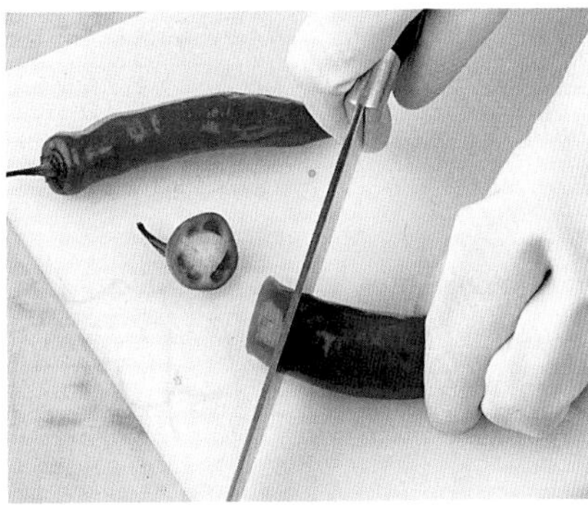

2. Peel the garlic. Chop the chillies, removing the seeds if a milder flavour is preferred.

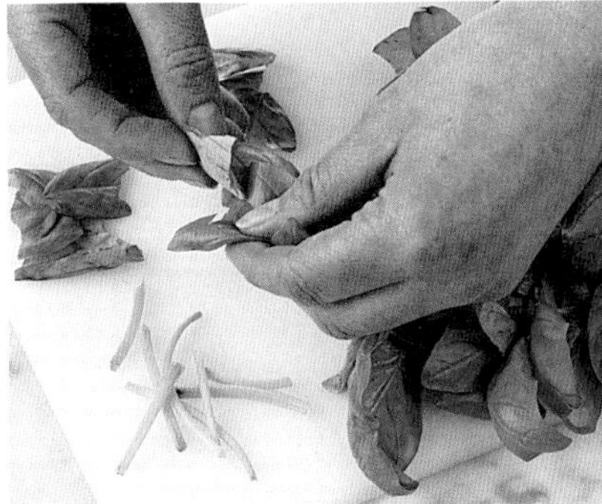

3. Remove and discard any thick, tough stems from the basil. Tear or cut any large leaves or stems into manageable pieces.

4. Put the nuts, garlic, chillies and basil leaves in a food processor and process until finely chopped. Add a little of the olive oil if the ingredients get stuck around the blades.

5. Now with the machine still running, slowly pour in the olive oil until the mixture is thick and creamy. Turn the mixture into a bowl and add a squeeze of lemon juice. Season to taste with salt and pepper. Store in a screw-topped jar in the refrigerator for up to 1 week.

MIXED SATAY

Satay sticks of tender meat and prawns make a great start to an informal meal – just be sure to make plenty as they are always popular. If preferred, use skinless chicken breast fillets in place of pork. The peanut sauce keeps well in the fridge so you can prepare it ahead, for convenience.

SERVES 6

350 g (12 oz) pork fillet
12 large raw prawns
350 g (12 oz) rump steak
squeeze of lemon juice
1 garlic clove, crushed
5 ml (1 tsp) salt
15 ml (1 tbsp) soft dark brown sugar
10 ml (2 tsp) ground coriander
10 ml (2 tsp) ground cumin
5 ml (1 tsp) turmeric
60 ml (4 tbsp) coconut milk
melted ghee, butter or oil, for brushing

PEANUT SAUCE

75 g (3 oz) roasted peanuts
1 garlic clove
30 ml (2 tbsp) Thai Red Curry Paste (see page 7)
400 ml (14 fl oz) coconut milk
pinch of hot chilli powder
30 ml (2 tbsp) soft dark brown sugar
squeeze of lemon juice

TO GARNISH

lime or lemon wedges

PREPARATION TIME
30 minutes, plus marinating
COOKING TIME
About 10 minutes
FREEZING
Not suitable

495 CALS PER SERVING

1. Cut the pork into 2.5 cm (1 inch) slices on the diagonal, along the length of the fillet. Put the pork slices between two sheets of cling film and, using a meat mallet or rolling pin, beat until fairly thin. Cut each slice into 2 or 3 strips, measuring about 2.5 cm (1 inch) across.

2. Peel the prawns, leaving the tail end attached. Using a small sharp knife, make a shallow slit along the outer curve from the tail to the head end and remove the dark intestinal vein. Wash under cold running water, then drain and dry with kitchen paper.

3. Cut the steak into thin strips, roughly the same size as the pork.

4. Put the meat and prawns in a shallow glass dish and sprinkle with the lemon juice. In a small bowl, mix the garlic with the salt, sugar and spices. Stir in the coconut milk to make a fairly dry paste.

5. Spoon the spice paste over the meat and prawns and rub it all over them. Cover and leave to marinate for at least 30 minutes, preferably overnight.

6. To make the peanut sauce, toast the peanuts under the grill, shaking the pan occasionally, to ensure that they brown evenly. Transfer to a food processor or blender and add the garlic, Thai curry paste and a little of the coconut milk to prevent the mixture sticking. Process until almost smooth. Add the rest of the coconut milk with the chilli powder, sugar and lemon juice. Work until evenly blended, then transfer to a saucepan.

7. Bring to the boil and cook for 2 minutes, then lower the heat and simmer gently for 10 minutes, stirring occasionally. If the mixture becomes too thick, thin with a little water.

8. Thread each prawn and piece of meat onto a bamboo skewer. Brush with ghee, butter or oil and cook under a very hot grill for about 10 minutes, turning frequently. The prawns should be opaque and their tails bright pink; the beef should be still just pink in the centre; the pork must be cooked right through.

9. Serve the satay on a platter, garnished with lime or lemon wedges and accompanied by the warm peanut sauce.

TECHNIQUE

Using your fingertips, rub the spice paste into the meat and prawns.

PAKORAS

In India these tasty fritters are made with a variety of vegetables, hard-boiled eggs or chicken. If making pakoras with root vegetables, you will need to parboil them first. As an alternative – or in addition – to the chutney suggested below, try serving pakoras with a refreshing raita made from yogurt and chopped fresh mint.

MAKES ABOUT 18

about 575 g (1 ¼ lb) prepared vegetables, such as onion, mushrooms, cauliflower, okra, aubergine, chillies
10 ml (2 tsp) cumin seeds
10 ml (2 tsp) coriander seeds
1-2 dried red chillies
30 ml (2 tbsp) vegetable oil
175 g (6 oz) gram flour
10 ml (2 tsp) garam masala
5 ml (1 tsp) salt
handful of fresh mint leaves (optional)

CORIANDER CHUTNEY

1 onion, peeled
1 garlic clove, peeled
2 hot red chillies
10 ml (2 tsp) sugar
5 ml (1 tsp) salt
30 ml (2 tbsp) lime or lemon juice
30 ml (2 tbsp) vegetable oil
15 ml (1 tbsp) ground almonds
2 canned or bottled red peppers, drained
1 large bunch of fresh coriander

PREPARATION TIME
40 minutes, plus standing
COOKING TIME
12-16 minutes
FREEZING
Suitable

75 CALS PER PAKORA

1. Cut the vegetables into smaller pieces as necessary: thickly slice the onion; divide cauliflower into small florets; cut aubergine into chunks or slices.

2. Crush the cumin, coriander seeds and dried chillies, using a pestle and mortar. Heat the oil in a frying pan, add the spice mixture and fry for 2 minutes, stirring.

3. Mix the gram flour, garam masala and salt together in a bowl. Add the spice mixture, then gradually stir in about 200 ml (7 fl oz) cold water or enough to make a thick batter. Beat vigorously with a wooden spoon or a balloon whisk to remove any lumps. Stir in the whole mint leaves, if using. Leave the batter to stand for about 30 minutes.

4. Meanwhile, make the chutney. Quarter the onion and place in a food processor or blender with all of the other ingredients, except the red peppers and a handful of coriander. Process until well mixed but still retaining some texture, then transfer to a bowl. Coarsely chop the red peppers and reserved coriander and stir into the chutney. Cover and leave to stand for 30 minutes to let the flavours develop.

5. Heat the oil in a deep-fat fryer to 190°C (375°F). Test the temperature by dropping a teaspoonful of batter into the oil – it should sizzle immediately on contact and rise to the surface.

6. When the oil is ready, cook the vegetables in batches. Dip a few pieces into the batter, then remove one piece at a time and carefully lower into the oil. Cook for about 4 minutes or until golden brown. Drain on crumpled kitchen paper. Repeat with the remaining vegetables, but don't try to cook too many pieces at one time or they will stick together.

7. Serve the pakoras piping hot, as soon as they are all cooked, accompanied by the coriander chutney.

NOTE: Gram flour is made from ground chick peas and has a unique flavour. It is well worth seeking out in Indian food stores or healthfood shops but if unobtainable you can use plain wholemeal flour instead, adding a little extra water.

TECHNIQUE

Deep-fry the pakoras, a few at a time, until golden brown and crisp. Drain on crumpled kitchen paper.

VEGETABLE SAMOSAS

If you're serving these as a starter, make a quick chutney to accompany them. Peel and finely slice a few spring onions, mix with a little crushed garlic, then toss with freshly torn mint and coriander leaves, a splash of lemon juice, a dash of oil and plenty of seasoning. Alternatively serve with mango chutney.

MAKES 24

450 g (1 lb) potatoes
salt and pepper
1 onion
1-2 hot green chillies
15 ml (1 tbsp) oil
1 garlic clove, crushed
10 ml (2 tsp) ground coriander
10 ml (2 tsp) cumin seeds
5 ml (1 tsp) ground fenugreek
1 large ripe tomato
50 g (2 oz) frozen peas
30 ml (2 tbsp) chopped fresh coriander
15 ml (1 tbsp) chopped fresh mint
oil for deep-frying
PASTRY
450 g (1 lb) plain white flour
5 ml (1 tsp) salt
45 ml (3 tbsp) chopped fresh coriander
60 ml (4 tbsp) vegetable oil, melted ghee or butter
TO GARNISH
mint sprigs
lime halves

PREPARATION TIME
45 minutes
COOKING TIME
About 15 minutes
FREEZING
Suitable

150 CALS PER SAMOSA

1. Peel and halve the potatoes. Cook in salted water until just tender. Drain and chop into fairly small pieces.

2. Peel and finely chop the onion. Chop the chilli(es), removing the seeds for a milder flavour. Heat the oil in a frying pan. Add the onion and garlic and cook for about 5 minutes until softened. Add the spices and cook for 2 minutes, stirring all the time.

3. Chop the tomato, add to the pan and simmer until softened. Add the potatoes and stir to coat in the spice mixture. Add the peas and cook for 1-2 minutes until thawed. Add the herbs and plenty of seasoning. Remove from heat; let cool.

4. To make the pastry, mix the flour, salt, and herbs if using, together in a bowl. Add the oil or melted fat and enough warm water to make a soft dough – about 200 ml (7 fl oz). Turn onto a lightly floured surface and knead for about 5 minutes.

5. Divide the dough into 12 pieces; keep covered with a damp cloth to prevent drying out. Roll one piece out to a 15 cm (6 inch) round, using a small plate as a guide or to neaten the edges if liked. Cut in half to make 2 semi-circles. Put a heaped teaspoon of filling on each semi-circle. Dampen the edges, fold over the filling and press together to seal. Repeat with remaining pastry and filling.

6. Heat the oil in a deep-fat fryer to 180°C (350°F). Test the temperature by dropping a small piece of pastry into the oil – the pastry should sizzle immediately on contact and rise to the surface.

7. Deep-fry the samosas, two or three at a time, for 3-5 minutes or until pale golden brown. Drain on crumpled kitchen paper. Serve warm, garnished with mint and lime halves.

MEAT SAMOSAS

Omit the potato. After frying the spices add 175 g (6 oz) minced lamb or beef and fry until browned. Add 5-10 ml (1-2 tsp) curry paste and a few spoonfuls of water and cook for about 20 minutes or until the meat is tender. Add the peas and cook for 2 minutes. Cool and complete as above.

TECHNIQUE

Dampen the edges of each semi-circle, fold to enclose the filling and press together firmly to seal.

SPICED PORK WONTONS

These powerfully flavoured meatballs are wrapped in a casing of shredded wonton pastry. Look for wonton wrappers in good Chinese supermarkets where they are invariably sold both fresh and frozen, or scour the 'ethnic' section of your local supermarket. Alternatively, try making your own wrappers (see note). Serve these wontons as cocktail nibbles or as a prelude to a stir-fried main course, accompanied by a soy sauce dip, flavoured with chopped chilli and sesame oil, if you like.

MAKES 20-24

2.5 cm (1 inch) piece fresh root ginger
2 garlic cloves
1 small onion
2 hot chillies
5 ml (1 tsp) Chinese five-spice powder
90 ml (6 tbsp) chopped fresh coriander
700 g (1 ½ lb) lean minced pork
salt and pepper
20-24 wonton wrappers
1 egg, beaten
oil for deep-frying

PREPARATION TIME
30 minutes
COOKING TIME
About 15 minutes
FREEZING
Not suitable

100 CALS PER WONTON

1. Peel the ginger and cut in half. Peel the garlic. Peel and quarter the onion. Remove the stems from the chillies and, if a milder flavour is preferred, discard the seeds. Put all of these ingredients in a food processor or blender and process until finely chopped.

2. Add the five-spice powder, coriander and pork. Process again until evenly mixed. Season generously with salt and pepper.

3. Using floured hands, shape the mixture into walnut-sized balls.

4. Wrap each one in a wonton wrapper, sealing the edges with beaten egg. Alternatively, stack the wonton wrappers in a neat pile and cut into thin shreds, using a large sharp knife. Spread them in a single layer on a plate. Dip the pork balls into the beaten egg then drop onto the shredded wontons and roll around on the plate until coated on all sides. The wonton strips should stick out, rather than lie flat.

5. Heat the oil in a deep-fat fryer to 175°C (345°F). Test the temperature by dropping in a cube of bread – it should turn golden brown in about 1 minute. Deep-fry the wontons, in batches, for about 4 minutes until golden brown on all sides and the pork is cooked right through. Drain on crumpled kitchen paper. Serve warm.

NOTE: To make your own wonton wrappers, put 225 g (8 oz) plain white flour in a bowl with a large pinch of salt. Beat 1 egg with 60 ml (4 tbsp) cold water and stir into the flour. Knead together with your fingers, adding a little more water if necessary to make a smooth dough. Cover with a damp cloth and leave to rest for 30 minutes. Roll out the dough *very* thinly and cut into 7.5 cm (3 inch) squares.

VARIATIONS

Replace the pork with minced lamb or chicken. Replace the fresh coriander with 4 finely chopped spring onions.

TECHNIQUE

Roll the pork balls around on the shredded wonton wrappers until coated on all sides.

DEEP-FRIED WHITEBAIT WITH HOT SAUCE

Whitebait are the young of herrings or sprats. Usually no more than about 5 cm (2 inches) long, they are eaten head, bones and all. Here they are deep-fried – always the best way to cook whitebait – and partnered by a fiery paprika and chilli sauce. Serve as a starter or lunch dish, or as part of a mezze or tapas-style meal comprising a variety of savoury dishes.

SERVES 4

700 g (1½ lb) whitebait
60 ml (4 tbsp) plain white flour
oil for deep-frying
HOT SAUCE
25 g (1 oz) ground hazelnuts
2-3 hot red chillies
1 small onion
3 garlic cloves
1 ripe tomato
15 ml (1 tbsp) mild paprika
salt and pepper
10 ml (2 tsp) balsamic or red wine vinegar
about 60 ml (4 tbsp) virgin olive oil
TO SERVE
chopped parsley, to garnish
paprika, for sprinkling
lime or lemon wedges

PREPARATION TIME
20 minutes
COOKING TIME
About 15 minutes
FREEZING
Not suitable

790 CALS PER SERVING

1. First make the sauce. Preheat the grill to medium. Spread the hazelnuts in the grill pan and toast until golden brown, shaking the pan occasionally to ensure that they brown evenly. Remove the stems from the chillies. Peel and quarter the onion; peel the garlic. Immerse the tomato in a bowl of boiling water for 15-30 seconds, then remove and peel away the skin.

2. Put all the sauce ingredients, except the olive oil, in a food processor or blender and process until smooth. Add a little of the olive oil if the mixture gets stuck around the blades. With the machine running, gradually add the olive oil in a thin stream through the feeder tube, to make a fairly thick sauce. Season with salt and pepper to taste.

3. Put the flour in a bowl and season generously with salt and pepper. Add the whitebait and toss to coat in the flour.

4. Heat the oil in a deep-fat fryer to 190°C (380°F). Test the temperature by dropping a cube of stale bread into the oil – the bread should sizzle immediately on contact with the oil, rise to the surface and become golden brown in about 30 seconds.

5. Deep-fry the fish in the hot oil in batches for about 3 minutes or until golden brown. Drain on crumpled kitchen paper and keep hot while cooking the remainder.

6. Serve the whitebait as soon as they are all cooked, garnished with chopped parsley and a sprinkling of paprika, and accompanied by lime wedges and the sauce.

VARIATION

If you're short of time, serve the whitebait with a spiced mayonnaise instead of the hot sauce. Flavour some homemade or good bought mayonnaise with grated lime rind, chopped chilli and chopped basil to taste.

TECHNIQUE

Toss the whitebait in the well-seasoned flour to coat evenly.

SPICED QUICK-FRIED PRAWNS

Large raw prawns are used to delicious effect in this quick starter. They are now readily obtainable from fish counters in larger supermarkets as well as fishmongers. If you are unable to find any, use fresh or frozen, cooked peeled prawns instead and buy the largest variety available. The accompanying potato ribbons are optional: slimmers may prefer to omit them – as this reduces the calorie content to 235 cals per serving.

SERVES 4

450 g (1 lb) large raw prawns (see note)
2.5 cm (1 inch) piece fresh root ginger
5 ml (1 tsp) turmeric
5-10 ml (1-2 tsp) hot chilli powder
10 ml (2 tsp) black mustard seeds
5 green cardamoms, crushed
1 garlic clove, crushed
50 g (2 oz) butter or ghee
90 ml (6 tbsp) coconut milk
salt and pepper
POTATO RIBBONS
1 large elongated potato
oil for deep-frying
coarse sea salt
paprika

PREPARATION TIME
About 20 minutes, plus marinating
COOKING TIME
About 20 minutes
FREEZING
Not suitable

440 CALS PER SERVING

1. Peel the prawns leaving the tail end attached. Using a small sharp knife, make a shallow slit along the outer curve from the tail to the head end and remove the dark vein. Rinse under cold running water, drain and pat dry with kitchen paper.

2. Peel and grate the ginger and put into a bowl with the turmeric, chilli powder, mustard seeds, cardamoms and garlic. Add the prawns, turn to coat with the spice mixture and leave to marinate for about 20 minutes.

3. To make the potato ribbons (if required), peel the potato and cut along its length into 5 mm (¼ inch) slices. Using a swivel potato peeler and working along the thin side of one slice of potato, pare wafer-thin strips. (They should not look like crisps – if they do, you are holding the potato the wrong way round!)

4. Heat the oil in a deep-fat fryer to 190°C (375°F). Test the temperature by dropping in a piece of potato – it should sizzle immediately on contact with the oil and rise to the surface.

5. Deep-fry a few potato strips at a time for 2-3 minutes, until golden brown and crisp. Drain on crumpled kitchen paper and sprinkle with a little coarse salt and paprika. Keep hot, while cooking the remainder and the prawns.

6. To cook the prawns, heat the butter or ghee in a frying pan until foaming. Add the prawns and cook very quickly, stirring all the time, for 2 minutes. Add the coconut milk and simmer for about 4 minutes until the prawns are pink and opaque. Season with salt and pepper.

7. Serve the prawns at once, accompanied by the potato ribbons if serving, and naan bread or poppadums if wished. Provide guests with finger bowls.

NOTE: If raw prawns are unobtainable, use cooked ones instead. Simmer in the coconut milk for 1-2 minutes only.

TECHNIQUE

Peel the prawns, leaving the small fan-like piece at the end of the tail attached.

THAI FISH CAKES

Bursting with the flavours of chillies, kaffir lime and lemon grass, these bear absolutely no resemblance to the traditional British fish cake and are definitely not for serving with chips and tartare sauce! Serve them on a bed of salad leaves as a starter or snack, accompanied by a crunchy salad of shredded cabbage, beansprouts and pepper strips, tossed in a soy-based dressing and sprinkled with toasted sesame seeds.

MAKES ABOUT 10

450 g (1 lb) white fish fillets, such as cod or haddock
4 kaffir lime leaves
30 ml (2 tbsp) chopped fresh coriander
15 ml (1 tbsp) nam pla (Thai fish sauce)
15 ml (1 tbsp) lime juice
30 ml (2 tbsp) Thai Red Curry Paste (see page 7)
salt and pepper
flour, for coating
oil for shallow-frying
TO SERVE
salad leaves
shredded spring onion
1 mild red chilli, sliced
lime halves

PREPARATION TIME
25 minutes
COOKING TIME
About 20 minutes
FREEZING
Suitable

100 CALS PER FISH CAKE

1. Remove any skin from the fish, then place the fish in a food processor or blender and work until smooth.

2. Finely chop the lime leaves and add to the fish with the coriander, nam pla, lime juice and red curry paste. Season with salt and pepper. Process until well mixed.

3. Using lightly floured hands, divide the mixture into about 10 pieces and shape each one into a cake, about 6 cm (2½ inches) in diameter.

4. Shallow-fry the fish cakes in batches. Heat a 1 cm (½ inch) depth of oil in a frying pan. Cook the fish cakes, a few at a time, for about 4 minutes each side. Drain on crumpled kitchen paper and keep hot while cooking the remainder.

5. Serve the fish cakes as soon as they are all cooked, on a bed of salad leaves scattered with shredded spring onion and chilli slices. Serve with lime halves.

NOTE: If you don't have time to make your own curry paste use ready-made Thai red curry paste, which is available in jars from large supermarkets and delicatessens.

TECHNIQUE

With lightly floured hands, shape the mixture into cakes, each about 6 cm (2½ inches) in diameter.

PRAWNS FRIED WITH GREENS

This is a good way to use those interesting greens sold in Chinese food stores. Pak choi is the one with the long, ribbed white stalks and dark green leaves which grow from a central root, rather like a head of celery. Baby pak choi – the mini variety – is good in this dish as it can be left whole for maximum visual impact. Chinese flowering cabbage has thin white stems, bright green leaves and tiny yellow flowers. Some supermarkets now stock Dutch-grown varieties of these Chinese vegetables.

SERVES 4-6

2 garlic cloves
1 lemon grass stalk
2 kaffir lime leaves
2 red shallots, or 1 small red onion
1-2 hot red chillies
4 cm (1½ inch) piece fresh root ginger
15 ml (1 tbsp) coriander seeds
75 g (3 oz) green beans
175 g (6 oz) mangetouts
450 g (1 lb) large raw prawns (see note)
1 small head of pak choi or Chinese flowering cabbage, or 2-3 baby pak choi (or a mixture)
30 ml (2 tbsp) vegetable oil
juice of 1 lime, or to taste
30 ml (2 tbsp) nam pla (Thai fish sauce)
lime halves, to garnish

PREPARATION TIME
20 minutes
COOKING TIME
About 10 minutes
FREEZING
Not suitable

195-130 CALS PER SERVING

1. Peel the garlic and slice thinly. Cut the lemon grass in half and bruise with a rolling pin. Tear the kaffir lime leaves into small pieces. Peel and thinly slice the shallots or onion. Slice the chillies, discarding the seeds if a milder flavour is preferred. Peel the ginger and cut into long, thin shreds. Crush the coriander seeds. Trim the beans and mangetouts.

2. Peel the prawns, leaving the tail end attached. Using a small sharp knife, make a shallow slit along the outer curve from the tail to the head end and remove the dark intestinal vein. Rinse under cold running water, drain and pat dry with kitchen paper.

3. Trim the pak choi or Chinese flowering cabbage, removing any discoloured leaves or damaged stems. Leave baby pak choi whole; tear other leaves into manageable pieces.

4. Heat the oil in a wok or large frying pan. Add the garlic, lemon grass, lime leaves, shallots, chillies, ginger and coriander seeds, and stir-fry for 2 minutes. Add the green beans and cook for 2 minutes. Add the prawns, mangetouts and pak choi or Chinese flowering cabbage and stir-fry for 2-3 minutes, until the vegetables are cooked but still crisp and the prawns are pink and opaque.

5. Add the nam pla and lime juice, and heat through for 1 minute. Serve immediately, while the vegetables are crisp.

NOTE: If raw prawns are unobtainable, use cooked ones instead. Add with the lime juice; heat through for 1 minute only.

VARIATION

Replace the prawns with skinned chicken breast fillets, cut into wafer-thin slices. Stir-fry with the beans at stage 4.

TECHNIQUE

Using a small sharp knife, make a shallow slit along the outer curve of each prawn from tail to head end and remove the dark intestinal vein.

GLAZED SALMON WITH SOY AND GINGER

Based on the Japanese teriyaki style of cooking, salmon fillets are marinated in a well flavoured mixture that makes a shiny glaze once the fish is grilled. Caledonian fillets – sold in most large supermarkets – are ideal for this dish. These are neat strips of boneless salmon cut across the grain. You can, of course, create your own by halving ordinary salmon fillets. Keeping the tone of the meal oriental, serve with deep-fried shredded seaweed or green cabbage sprinkled with toasted sesame seeds, and/or a pile of finely shredded mooli (white radish).

SERVES 4

- **6 cm (2½ inch) piece fresh root ginger**
- **1 garlic clove (optional)**
- **90 ml (6 tbsp) light soy sauce**
- **120 ml (8 tbsp) mirin (Japanese rice wine) or sweet sherry**
- **15 ml (1 tbsp) soft brown sugar**
- **8 Caledonian salmon fillets, or 4 salmon fillets, each about 175 g (6 oz)**

PREPARATION TIME
20 minutes, plus marinating
COOKING TIME
About 8-10 minutes
FREEZING
Not suitable

400 CALS PER SERVING

1. Peel the ginger, and garlic if using. Crush both using a pestle and mortar, or a rolling pin and a strong bowl, until the juices start to run. Then, using your hands, squeeze out as much of the juice as possible into a shallow dish, taking care to exclude any solid pieces of ginger or garlic (as these would burn during cooking and spoil the effect).

2. Put the soy sauce, mirin or sherry and the sugar into a small saucepan and dissolve over a low heat, then bring to the boil, stirring all the time. Boil for about 5 minutes until the mixture is slightly reduced and syrupy. Pour onto the ginger juice and leave to cool completely.

3. Add the fish to the dish and turn to coat with the marinade on all sides. Leave to marinate in a cool place for 30 minutes to 1 hour.

4. Preheat the grill to high. Thread each piece of fish onto two long bamboo skewers. Thoroughly oil the grill pan and lay the fish in the pan, skin-side down. Grill for about 6-8 minutes or until the fish flakes easily when tested with a fork, brushing frequently during cooking with the excess marinade. If the salmon appears to be overcooking on the surface but not cooking underneath, lower the position of the grill pan rather than turn the fish over. Serve immediately.

VARIATIONS

Mackerel: Use 2 filleted fresh mackerel. Marinate and cook as above, for 6-10 minutes depending on thickness.
Beef: Use thick slices of rump steak. Marinate and cook as above, for about 5 minutes each side. Cut into neat thick slices to serve.
Chicken: Use breast fillets. Flatten slightly between sheets of cling film. Marinate and cook as above, for about 12-15 minutes, turning occasionally. Serve cut into neat slices.

TECHNIQUE

Carefully thread each piece of salmon onto two long bamboo skewers.

MUSSELS WITH SPICED COCONUT BROTH

Mussels are at their best from September through to April – when there is an 'r' in the month. Frozen ones are available but nothing quite compares with a plate of steaming freshly cooked mussels. They are best bought fresh from a good fishmonger and eaten on the day of purchase. Always make sure that you clean them properly, following the instructions below, and be ruthless about discarding those which refuse to open.

SERVES 4

1.8 kg (4 lb) fresh mussels in the shell
1 small onion
1-2 garlic cloves
2-3 dried red chillies
30 ml (2 tbsp) vegetable oil
15 ml (1 tbsp) ground coriander
2 lemon grass stalks
handful of fresh coriander leaves
5 cm (2 inch) piece of fresh or dried galangal
6 kaffir lime leaves
300 ml (½ pint) coconut milk
salt and pepper

PREPARATION TIME
About 20 minutes
COOKING TIME
15 minutes
FREEZING
Not suitable

405 CALS PER SERVING

1. To prepare the mussels, scrub them under cold running water, scraping off any mud, barnacles or seaweed with a small sharp knife. Pull or cut off the hairy 'beard' protruding from the shell. Discard any mussels with cracked or broken shells or any that refuse to close when tapped with the back of the knife. Put the mussels in a colander and set aside.

2. To make the broth, peel and finely chop the onion and garlic. Crumble the chillies. Heat the oil in a large saucepan, add the onion, garlic and chillies and sauté for about 5 minutes until the onion is softened. Add the ground coriander and cook for 1 minute, stirring all the time.

3. Cut each lemon grass stalk in half and bruise with a rolling pin. Roughly chop half of the coriander leaves. Thinly slice the galangal. Add these ingredients to the onion mixture with the lime leaves. Stir in the coconut milk and 150 ml (¼ pint) water. Bring to the boil, lower the heat and simmer gently for 10 minutes. Season carefully with salt and pepper.

4. Add the mussels to the broth, then cover the pan with a tight-fitting lid. Simmer gently for about 5 minutes, shaking the pan from time to time, until the mussels open. Discard any unopened ones. Do not overcook or the mussels will be tough.

5. Spoon the mussels into deep serving bowls and scatter with the reserved coriander. Serve with plenty of bread or bowls of plain rice to mop up the delicious broth once the mussels have been eaten. Don't forget to provide a bowl for discarded shells and plenty of napkins.

VARIATION

For a tomato-based broth replace the coconut milk with a 425 g (15 oz) can chopped tomatoes.

TECHNIQUE

Clean the mussels thoroughly under cold running water, removing the hairy 'beard' that protrudes from each shell.

MEE GORENG

This sumptuous dish is on the menu of one of my favourite Malaysian restaurants and I've been trying to emulate it ever since I first savoured it there many years ago! For a less elaborate dish you can simply omit the squid and replace the raw prawns with cooked peeled prawns – increasing the weight to 225 g (8 oz).

SERVES 4-6

125 g (4 oz) rump steak
2 garlic cloves, crushed
30 ml (2 tbsp) soy sauce
450 g (1 lb) squid
175 g (6 oz) large raw prawns
225 g (8 oz) medium egg noodles
salt
1-2 hot red chillies
2.5 cm (1 inch) piece fresh root ginger
2-3 spring onions
15 ml (1 tbsp) vegetable oil
15 ml (1 tbsp) sesame or peanut oil
30 ml (2 tbsp) hoisin sauce
15 ml (1 tbsp) lemon juice
30 ml (2 tbsp) nam pla (Thai fish sauce)
125 g (4 oz) beansprouts
TO GARNISH
shredded lettuce
lemon wedges

PREPARATION TIME
30 minutes
COOKING TIME
About 10 minutes
FREEZING
Not suitable

475-315 CALS PER SERVING

1. Cut the steak into wafer-thin slices across the grain. Place in a shallow dish with half of the garlic and half of the soy sauce. Leave to stand.

2. Rinse the squid then, holding the body in one hand, firmly pull the tentacles with the other hand to remove the soft contents of the body. Cut the tentacles just in front of the eyes and discard the body contents. Cut the tentacles into small pieces.

3. Squeeze out the plastic-like quill from the body and discard. Rinse the body under cold running water, making sure that it is clean inside. Rub off the fine dark skin, then cut the body into rings or small rectangular pieces.

4. Peel the prawns, leaving the tail end attached. Using a small sharp knife, make a shallow slit along the outer curve from the tail to the head end and remove the dark intestinal vein. Rinse under cold running water, drain and pat dry with kitchen paper.

5. Put the noodles in a large saucepan with a generous pinch of salt and pour over enough boiling water to cover. Bring to the boil and turn off the heat. Leave to stand and cook in the residual heat according to the packet instructions, while cooking the seafood.

6. Chop the chillies, discarding the seeds if a milder flavour is preferred. Peel and finely chop the ginger. Trim and slice the spring onions. Heat the oils in a wok or large frying pan, add the remaining garlic, chillies, ginger and spring onions, and cook for 2 minutes, stirring all the time.

7. Add the marinated beef and cook for 2 minutes. Add the squid and prawns and cook for 2 minutes. Add the hoisin sauce, lemon juice, nam pla and remaining soy sauce and cook for 2 minutes.

8. Drain the noodles and add to the pan with the beansprouts. Heat through for a couple of minutes, then add the beaten egg. Cook briefly until the egg is on the point of setting, then remove from the heat. Serve at once, garnishing each portion with a mound of shredded lettuce and a lemon wedge.

TECHNIQUE

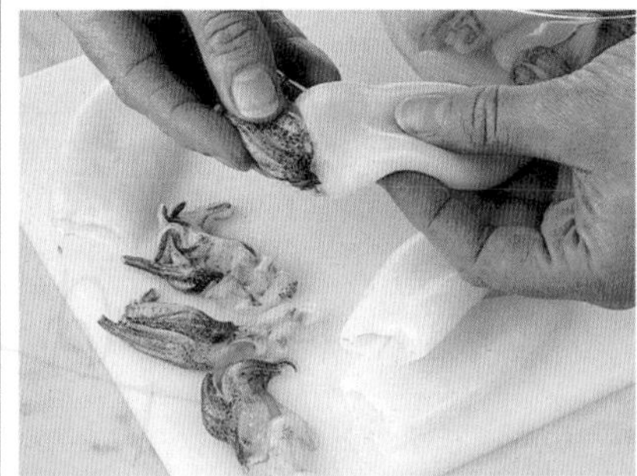

Holding the body of the squid in one hand, firmly pull the body and the tentacles apart. The soft contents of the body will emerge with the tentacles.

GREEN CURRY OF FISH AND SEAFOOD

If you're squeamish, you may prefer to look out for ready-prepared fresh or frozen baby squid. But don't be put off – the preparation is easy and it isn't nearly as unpleasant as it sounds! I find the best place for this is in the sink with the cold tap running. Whatever you do, don't overcook squid, otherwise it will be tough and live up to its rubbery reputation.

SERVES 4-6

350 g (12 oz) squid
350 g (12 oz) medium raw prawns
450 g (1 lb) firm white fish fillets, such as cod, haddock, halibut, monkfish
few mussels or clams (optional)
15 ml (1 tbsp) vegetable oil
45 ml (3 tbsp) Green Curry Paste (see page 8)
1 lemon grass stalk
few kaffir lime leaves, shredded
450 ml (¾ pint) coconut milk
30 ml (2 tbsp) nam pla (Thai fish sauce)
squeeze of lime juice
chopped coriander, to garnish

PREPARATION TIME
30 minutes
COOKING TIME
About 10 minutes
FREEZING
Not suitable

610-410 CALS PER SERVING

1. Rinse the squid then, holding the body in one hand, firmly pull the tentacles with the other hand (see technique, page 30). As you do so, the soft contents of the body will come out. Cut the tentacles just in front of the eyes and discard the body contents. Cut the tentacles into small pieces.

2. Squeeze out the plastic-like quill from the body and discard. Rinse the body under cold running water, making sure that it is clean inside. Rub off the fine dark skin, then cut the body into rings or small rectangular pieces.

3. Peel the raw prawns, leaving the small fan-like piece at the end of the tail attached. Using a small sharp knife, make a shallow slit along the outer curve from the tail to the head end and remove the dark intestinal vein. Rinse under cold running water, drain and pat dry with kitchen paper.

4. Cut the white fish fillets into large pieces. Prepare the mussels if using (following the instructions on page 28). If using clams, prepare in the same way.

5. Heat the oil in a large frying pan, add the curry paste and cook for 2 minutes, stirring all the time. Bruise the lemon grass and add to the pan with the shredded lime leaves. Add the coconut milk and bring to the boil, stirring.

6. Reduce the heat to a simmer, then add the white fish, prawns and squid. Cook for 1-2 minutes until they look opaque. Add the mussels or clams if using, cover with a lid or a baking sheet and simmer for a few minutes until the shells have opened. Discard any that remain closed.

7. Flavour with the nam pla and lime juice and serve immediately, garnished with chopped coriander.

TECHNIQUE

Squeeze out the plastic-like quill from the body of the squid and discard.

FISH BAKED WITH HOT SPICES

Make this simple dish with your favourite fish – it works well with any firm white fish, such as cod, haddock, monkfish or sea bass. Oily fish, like salmon, trout and mackerel, are not suitable. While the fish is marinating, make a tabbouleh salad to serve with it (see below).

SERVES 4

4 large white fish fillets, such as cod, haddock, monkfish, sea bass, each 175 g (6 oz)
SPICE MIXTURE
3 garlic cloves, crushed
grated rind and juice of 1 lemon
grated rind of 1 lime
30 ml (2 tbsp) chopped fresh coriander
30 ml (2 tbsp) chopped fresh parsley
large pinch of powdered saffron
large pinch of turmeric
5 ml (1 tsp) ground cumin
2.5 ml (½ tsp) ground cinnamon
5-10 ml (1-2 tsp) hot chilli sauce
10 ml (2 tsp) brown sugar
15 ml (1 tbsp) sweet paprika
60 ml (4 tbsp) olive oil
salt and pepper

PREPARATION TIME
15 minutes, plus marinating
COOKING TIME
10-15 minutes
FREEZING
Not suitable

280 CALS PER SERVING

1. Combine all the ingredients for the spice mixture in a glass bowl, adding plenty of salt and pepper. Whisk together with a fork.

2. Rub the spice mixture into the fish fillets, making sure that each piece is completely coated. Leave to marinate in a cool place for 30 minutes to 1 hour. Don't be tempted to leave it much longer than this, or the acid in the marinade will begin to 'cook' the fish.

3. Preheat the oven to 200°C (400°F) Mark 6. Wrap each fish fillet in a piece of foil and place on a baking sheet. Bake in the oven for about 10-15 minutes or until the fish flakes easily when tested with a fork. The cooking time will depend on the thickness of the fillets: if using chunky fillets like monkfish or cod they will take longer than thinner, more delicate fillets.

4. Unwrap and transfer each fillet to a warmed serving plate. Pour the liquid from each parcel over the fish. Serve at once, with a tabbouleh salad.

TABBOULEH SALAD

Put 175 g (6 oz) bulgar wheat in a bowl and pour on boiling water to cover and come about 1 cm (½ inch) above. Leave to soak for about 20 minutes or until all the water has been absorbed and the wheat has softened.

Meanwhile, finely chop about 4 ripe juicy tomatoes, 6 spring onions or 1 small red onion, a large handful of fresh parsley and a large handful of fresh mint. Add these to the soaked wheat and season generously with salt, pepper and ground allspice. Add olive oil and lemon juice to taste. Toss lightly to mix – the finished effect should be quite green.

TECHNIQUE

Spoon the spice mixture onto the fish fillets, then rub well in to ensure that each piece is completely coated.

THAI SOUP

An authentic Thai dish, heady with the scent and flavour of lemon grass and galangal. Don't despair about the availability of Thai ingredients: some of the larger supermarket chains now offer a Thai spice pack alongside their fresh herbs. This main course soup is best eaten with a spoon and chopsticks.

SERVES 4

225 g (8 oz) firm tofu
vegetable oil, for shallow or deep-frying
125 g (4 oz) thin or medium egg noodles
300 g (10 oz) cooked chicken, skinned
2.5 cm (1 inch) piece fresh root ginger
2.5 cm (1 inch) piece fresh or dried galangal (optional)
1-2 garlic cloves
2 lemon grass stalks
175 g (6 oz) cauliflower florets
1 large carrot
few green beans
3 spring onions
5 ml (1 tsp) chilli powder
2.5 ml (½ tsp) turmeric
600 ml (1 pint) coconut milk
600 ml (1 pint) chicken or vegetable stock, or water
75 g (3 oz) bean sprouts
125 g (4 oz) peeled prawns (optional)
30 ml (2 tbsp) soy sauce

PREPARATION TIME
20 minutes
COOKING TIME
About 20 minutes
FREEZING
Not suitable

690-460 CALS PER SERVING

1. Pat the tofu dry with kitchen paper, then cut into small cubes. Heat the oil in a wok or deep-fat fryer and fry the tofu, in batches, until golden brown on all sides. Drain on kitchen paper.

2. Put the noodles in a large saucepan with a good pinch of salt and pour over enough boiling water to cover. Bring to the boil, then turn off the heat. Leave to stand and allow the noodles to cook in the residual heat according to the packet instructions.

3. Cut the chicken into bite-sized pieces. Peel and finely chop the ginger. Finely slice the galangal. Crush the garlic. Halve each lemon grass stalk and bruise with a rolling pin or the heel of your hand.

4. Break the cauliflower into tiny florets, thinly slicing any thick stems. Peel the carrot and cut into matchstick strips or thin slices. Trim and halve the beans. Trim and finely slice the spring onions.

5. Heat 30 ml (2 tbsp) vegetable oil in a large saucepan. Add the ginger, galangal, garlic, lemon grass, chilli powder, turmeric and chicken and cook for 2 minutes, stirring all the time. Add the cauliflower and carrot.

6. Add the coconut milk and stock and bring to the boil, stirring. Reduce heat and simmer for 10 minutes. Add the beans and simmer for 5 minutes.

7. Drain the noodles and add to the soup with the prawns if using, tofu, spring onions, beansprouts and soy sauce. Simmer gently for 5 minutes or until heated through. Serve immediately, in deep soup bowls.

TECHNIQUE

To prepare the flavouring ingredients, peel and finely chop the ginger; finely slice the galangal; crush the garlic; halve and crush the lemon grass stalks.

CHICKEN FAJITAS

Serve this Mexican-style dish with tortillas, guacamole and plenty of soured cream. If you have trouble buying ready-made corn tortillas you could always make your own wheat version (see below).

SERVES 6

3 onions
2-3 hot chillies
2 garlic cloves, crushed
30 ml (2 tbsp) chopped fresh coriander
grated rind and juice of 2 limes
6 chicken breast fillets, skinned
8 red, yellow or orange peppers (or a mixture)
15-30 ml (1-2 tbsp) olive oil
salt and pepper
TO SERVE
coriander leaves, to garnish
12 tortillas
guacamole (optional)
soured cream

PREPARATION TIME
30 minutes, plus marinating
COOKING TIME
About 15 minutes
FREEZING
Not suitable

335 CALS PER SERVING

1. Peel and halve the onions, leaving most of the root end attached so that they will hold their shape during cooking. Cut each half into wedges, working from the root end to the top. Slice the chillies, discarding the seeds if a milder flavour is preferred.

2. Put the garlic, onions, chillies, chopped coriander, lime rind and juice in a shallow dish and mix thoroughly. Cut the chicken into large pieces and add to the dish. Stir well, cover and leave to marinate in a cool place for at least 1 hour or overnight.

3. Halve the peppers and remove the cores and seeds, then cut into wedges.

4. Heat the oil in a heavy-based frying pan. Remove the chicken and onions from the marinade with a slotted spoon, reserving the marinade. Add the chicken and onions to the pan and cook, turning, over a high heat until thoroughly browned on the outside. Remove the chicken from the pan.

5. Add the peppers to the pan and cook, turning, over a high heat for about 5 minutes until the onions and peppers are softened.

6. Return the chicken to the pan, add the marinade, lower the heat and cook for about 5 minutes, stirring occasionally, or until the chicken is cooked right through.

7. Season with salt and pepper to taste and sprinkle with the coriander leaves. Serve immediately, with the tortillas, guacamole if desired, and plenty of soured cream.

HOMEMADE TORTILLAS

Put 300 g (10 oz) plain white flour in a food processor with 7.5 ml (1½ tsp) salt and 50 g (2 oz) white vegetable fat. Process briefly then, with the machine running, gradually add 150-175 ml (5-6 fl oz) warm water or enough to make a fairly soft dough. Knead briefly on a floured surface, then divide into 12 pieces. Roll out each piece to an 18 cm (7 inch) circle. Cook the tortillas one at a time on an ungreased griddle or frying pan for 1 minute each side.

TECHNIQUE

Add the chicken to the onions, garlic, chillies, coriander and lime. Stir to mix thoroughly.

CHICKEN VINDALOO

This fiery curry originates from Southern India where it is more usually made with lamb or beef. You can of course use lamb, beef or pork instead of chicken as long as you adjust the cooking times accordingly. However I find that this chicken version is most popular. It is intended to be hot so don't stint on the chillies – if yours are mild, add more! Serve with fluffy basmati rice, naan bread and a spicy vegetable accompaniment.

SERVES 4

900 g (2 lb) chicken pieces, such as thighs, drumsticks and breast fillets
2 onions
60 ml (4 tbsp) ghee or vegetable oil
6 garlic cloves
2.5 cm (1 inch) piece fresh root ginger
10 ml (2 tsp) cumin seeds
10 ml (2 tsp) coriander seeds
10 ml (2 tsp) fenugreek seeds
10 ml (2 tsp) black peppercorns
5 ml (1 tsp) turmeric
10 ml (2 tsp) sugar
2.5 ml (½ tsp) salt
60 ml (4 tbsp) red or white wine vinegar
8 green cardamoms
1 cinnamon stick
4-6 dried hot red chillies
30 ml (2 tbsp) tomato purée

PREPARATION TIME
20 minutes
COOKING TIME
About 1 hour
FREEZING
Suitable

330 CALS PER SERVING

1. Remove any skin from the chicken and cut any large portions in half.

2. Peel and chop the onions. Heat 30 ml (2 tbsp) of the ghee or oil in a frying pan. Add the onions and cook over a fairly high heat until golden brown, stirring all the time. Remove from the pan with a slotted spoon and drain on kitchen paper.

3. Peel the garlic cloves and ginger. Put these in a blender or food processor with the onions, cumin, coriander, fenugreek, peppercorns, turmeric, sugar, salt and vinegar. Process until smooth, then mix with the cardamoms, cinnamon and chillies.

4. Heat the remaining 30 ml (2 tbsp) ghee or vegetable oil in a large saucepan or casserole. Cook the chicken, in batches, until sealed on all sides. Add the vindaloo paste and stir so that the chicken is coated on all sides. Cook over a fairly high heat for about 5 minutes, stirring occasionally.

5. Add the tomato purée and 300 ml (½ pint) water. Bring to the boil, then lower the heat, cover and simmer gently for about 45 minutes or until the chicken is very tender. Check from time to time to make sure that the sauce hasn't evaporated completely – if it looks too dry, simply add a little more water. If the chicken is cooked and the sauce is too thin, just cook it over a high heat for a few minutes to boil off some of the liquid. Check the seasoning before serving, with rice.

VARIATIONS

Replace the chicken with lamb, beef or pork, adjusting the cooking times accordingly.

TECHNIQUE

Add the vindaloo paste to the chicken and stir to ensure that each piece of chicken is well coated.

CHICKEN BAKED WITH SPICES

This is a really easy, tasty supper dish. If you can, set the chicken to marinate the day before to allow plenty of time for it to absorb the flavourings. It will then be ready to pop into the oven when required. Serve with a simple rice pilaff and a crisp green salad.

SERVES 6

2 garlic cloves
30 ml (2 tbsp) mild paprika
10 ml (2 tsp) ground coriander
5-10 ml (1-2 tsp) cayenne pepper
finely grated rind and juice of 1 large lemon
30 ml (2 tbsp) chopped fresh mint
30 ml (2 tbsp) chopped fresh coriander
45 ml (3 tbsp) grated fresh coconut (optional)
200 ml (7 fl oz) thick yogurt
salt and pepper
6 chicken suprêmes, or other portions
ghee, butter or vegetable oil, for brushing
TO SERVE
mint and rocket leaves
grated fresh coconut (optional)
lemon or lime wedges

PREPARATION TIME
15 minutes, plus marinating
COOKING TIME
About 25 minutes
FREEZING
Not suitable

260 CALS PER SERVING

1. Crush the garlic and mash with the paprika, coriander, cayenne pepper and lemon rind and juice. Put the herbs, and coconut if using, in a bowl and stir in the yogurt. Beat in the garlic mixture. Add salt and pepper to taste.

2. Skin each chicken suprême or portion and make 2 or 3 deep cuts in the thickest part of the flesh.

3. Drop the chicken portions into the yogurt mixture and turn the portions in the mixture so that they are thoroughly coated on all sides. Make sure that the marinade goes well into the slashes. Leave to marinate in a cool place for at least 30 minutes, or overnight if possible.

4. Preheat the oven to 200°C (400°F) Mark 6. Arrange the chicken in a single layer in a roasting tin and brush with melted butter, ghee or oil. Roast in the oven, basting from time to time, for about 25 minutes until the chicken is cooked right through. To test it, pierce the thickest part with the point of a knife: if the juices run clear, the chicken is cooked; if there is any trace of pink, bake for a further 10 minutes.

5. Serve garnished with mint and rocket leaves, grated coconut if using, and lemon or lime wedges.

VARIATIONS

To simplify the recipe, replace the spices with 30 ml (2 tbsp) ready-made tandoori paste. If fresh herbs are unavailable, use 5 ml (1 tsp) mint concentrate instead.

TECHNIQUE

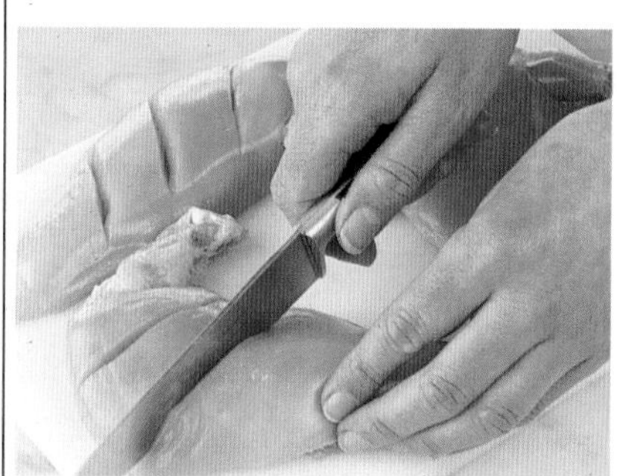

Make 2 or 3 deep slashes in each chicken suprême to enable the marinade to penetrate.

DUCK WITH HOT SAUCE AND TANGERINE

Tender duck breast fillets are browned over a high heat, then simmered briefly in fresh tangerine juice flavoured with spices. Serve this quick and easy dish on a bed of robust dark green salad leaves, such as baby spinach, rocket or watercress. Alternatively, accompany with plain boiled rice or crispy sautéed potatoes.

SERVES 3-4

2 large duck breast fillets, skinned
1-2 hot red chillies
1 garlic clove
2-3 juicy tangerines or satsumas
about 30 ml (2 tbsp) olive oil
1.25 ml (¼ tsp) ground ginger
5 ml (1 tsp) Moroccan Spice Mixture (see page 9)
1 cinnamon stick
150 ml (¼ pint) chicken stock
15 ml (1 tbsp) red wine vinegar
50 g (2 oz) green beans
50 g (2 oz) mangetouts
few asparagus tips (optional)
salt and pepper
tangerine halves, to garnish

PREPARATION TIME
10 minutes
COOKING TIME
About 20 minutes
FREEZING
Not suitable

290-215 CALS PER SERVING

1. Cut the duck into large pieces. Slice the chillies, removing the seeds if a milder flavour is preferred. Peel and slice the garlic.

2. Finely pare the rind and squeeze the juice from 2 tangerines. Measure 150 ml (¼ pint) juice, squeezing the third tangerine if necessary.

3. Heat the oil in a large heavy-based frying pan or casserole. Cook the duck in batches, over a very high heat, until thoroughly browned on the outside; remove from the pan and set aside.

4. Add a little more oil to the pan if necessary. Add the chilli(es) and garlic and cook gently for 1-2 minutes without browning. Add the ginger and spice mixture to the pan and cook for 1 minute.

5. Add the cinnamon stick, pared tangerine rind and juice, stock and vinegar. Bring to the boil, stirring to scrape up any sediment from the base of the pan.

6. Return the duck to the pan, with any accumulated juices. Cover and simmer very gently for 5 minutes, or until the duck is tender but still pink in the centre.

7. Meanwhile, trim the beans, mangetouts, and asparagus if using. Blanch in a pan of boiling salted water for 2 minutes. Drain thoroughly.

8. Add the vegetables to the sauce and heat through for 1 minute. Season to taste with salt and pepper. Remove the duck and vegetables from the pan using a slotted spoon, and arrange on serving plates. Boil the cooking juices for 2-3 minutes until reduced and syrupy, then pour over the duck. Serve immediately, garnished with tangerine halves.

VARIATION

Replace the duck with pork fillet or tenderloin. Cut the meat into thin slices and cook as above but make sure it is cooked through in step 6.

TECHNIQUE

Fry the pieces of duck in batches over a very high heat until thoroughly browned on the outside.

PASTA WITH CHORIZO

Chorizo is a spicy Spanish sausage, liberally flavoured and coloured with paprika. It is available both raw by the piece, and cured ready to slice and eat. If you are unable to buy it raw in one piece, use cured chorizo – sold pre-packed in supermarkets – and cook in the sauce for 5 minutes only. A robust red wine is the ideal accompaniment to this rustic dish.

SERVES 4-6

1 onion
2 garlic cloves
30 ml (2 tbsp) olive oil
30 ml (2 tbsp) tomato purée
30 ml (2 tbsp) mild paprika
1 dried chilli
2 bay leaves
2 fresh thyme sprigs
2 fresh rosemary sprigs
150 ml (¼ pint) dry red wine
425 g (15 oz) can chopped tomatoes
salt and pepper
450 g (1 lb) raw chorizo sausage, in one piece
400-450 g (14 oz-1 lb) fresh or dried pasta
chopped parsley, to garnish

PREPARATION TIME
10 minutes
COOKING TIME
About 50 minutes
FREEZING
Suitable

950-630 CALS PER SERVING

1. Peel and finely chop the onion. Crush the garlic. Heat the oil in a heavy-based saucepan, add the onion and garlic and sauté for about 5 minutes or until softened. Add the tomato purée and paprika and cook for 2 minutes, stirring all the time.

2. Crumble in the chilli, then add the bay leaves, thyme and rosemary. Pour in the wine and bring to the boil. Cook for 2 minutes, stirring. Add the tomatoes with their juice and bring to the boil again. Lower the heat and simmer gently for 30 minutes. Season generously with salt and pepper.

3. Cut the chorizo sausage into thick slices and add to the sauce. Cook for 15 minutes.

4. Meanwhile bring a large pan of boiling salted water to the boil. Add the pasta, bring back to the boil and stir once. Cook until *al dente*, tender but firm to the bite. Dried pasta will take about 10-12 minutes; fresh pasta 1-5 minutes.

5. Drain the pasta in a colander, shaking it vigorously to remove all water. Divide between warmed individual serving bowls or turn into a large warmed serving bowl. Spoon the sauce on top of the pasta, sprinkle with plenty of chopped parsley and serve immediately.

TECHNIQUE

Add the pasta to the boiling water and stir once to ensure it doesn't stick together.

LAMB BIRYANI

Biryani is a spectacular celebratory Indian dish of curried meat – lamb in this instance – and saffron-flecked rice. Although I've simplified things somewhat, it does take time to prepare.. To complete the meal, serve a lightly spiced vegetable dish, a fresh chutney and a yogurt raita.

SERVES 6

450 g (1 lb) white basmati rice
salt
1 large onion
3 garlic cloves
6 cm (2½ inch) piece fresh root ginger
25 g (1 oz) flaked almonds
15 ml (1 tbsp) ground coriander
10 ml (2 tsp) ground cumin
5 ml (1 tsp) ground fenugreek
700 g (1½ lb) boned leg or shoulder of lamb
90 ml (6 tbsp) ghee or oil
1 cinnamon stick
6 green cardamoms
6 cloves
150 ml (¼ pint) thick yogurt
5 ml (1 tsp) cayenne pepper
freshly grated nutmeg
5 ml (1 tsp) saffron strands
pinch of turmeric
40 g (1½ oz) butter
TO GARNISH
hard-boiled eggs, sultanas, toasted almonds, garam masala, coriander sprigs and crisp-fried onions (see note)

PREPARATION TIME
20 minutes, plus soaking rice
COOKING TIME
About 2 hours
FREEZING
Not suitable

740 CALS PER SERVING

1. Wash the rice in a sieve under cold running water until the water runs clear. Tip into a bowl, add 15 ml (1 tbsp) salt and enough water to cover. Leave to soak for about 1 hour.

2. Peel the onion and cut into quarters. Peel the garlic. Peel and roughly chop the ginger. Put the onion, garlic, ginger, almonds and ground spices in a food processor or blender. Add 15 ml (1 tbsp) water and purée until smooth.

3. Trim the lamb of any excess fat and cut into 2.5 cm (1 inch) cubes. Heat the ghee or oil in a large flameproof casserole. Brown the lamb in batches over a high heat, adding more ghee or oil as necessary. Remove from the pan; set aside.

4. Add the onion and spice paste to the pan and cook over a fairly high heat for about 5 minutes until the paste is golden brown, stirring all the time. Add the whole spices and cook for a further 2 minutes. Return all the meat to the pan and stir to coat in the onion and spices.

5. Lower the heat and gradually add the yogurt a spoonful at a time, stirring constantly. Add 150 ml (¼ pint) water, bring to a gentle simmer and cook for about 1 hour or until the meat is tender. Season with salt, cayenne and nutmeg. Cover with a tight-fitting lid and keep warm in a low oven set at 150°C (300°F) Mark 2 while cooking the rice.

6. Meanwhile, put the saffron in a small bowl with the turmeric and 60 ml (4 tbsp) warm water; leave to soak.

7. Drain the rice. Add to a large pan of boiling salted water, stir with a fork, then bring back to the boil and cook for 5 minutes. Drain thoroughly.

8. Pile the rice on top of the meat. Drizzle the saffron liquid across the rice and dot with the butter. Cover the casserole with a double thickness of foil, then the lid. Bake in the oven for 45 minutes.

9. To serve, transfer to a platter, fluff the rice carefully with a fork and garnish with eggs, sultanas, almonds, garam masala, coriander and the crisp onions.

NOTE: For the crisp-fried onion garnish, fry 2 sliced large onions in oil until dark golden brown. Drain on kitchen paper.

TECHNIQUE

Gradually stir the yogurt into the meat mixture, a spoonful at a time.

MOROCCAN LAMB WITH LEMONS AND OLIVES

A North African speciality with an intense lemony flavour. Adjust the strength of the flavour once the casserole is cooked – it will depend on the size of your lemons. Equally it is important to use really fresh spices for the Moroccan spice mixture – stale ones will not give the same depth of flavour.

SERVES 6

1.4 kg (3 lb) boned leg or shoulder of lamb
2 large onions
3 large lemons
45 ml (3 tbsp) olive oil
45 ml (3 tbsp) Moroccan Spice Mixture (see page 9)
1 large bunch of flat-leaved parsley
salt and pepper
225 g (8 oz) green olives
1 red onion, to garnish

PREPARATION TIME
15 minutes
COOKING TIME
1½-2 hours
FREEZING
Suitable

715 CALS PER SERVING

1. Trim the lamb of any excess fat and cut into 5 cm (2 inch) cubes. Peel and roughly chop the onions.

2. Pare a strip of rind from 1 lemon. Cut into shreds and set aside for the garnish.

3. Heat the oil in a flameproof casserole. Add the onions and cook over a fairly high heat for 2 minutes; remove from the pan. Quickly fry the meat in batches over a very high heat until nicely browned all over. Return all the meat and the onions to the casserole.

4. Add the spice mixture and cook, stirring all the time, for 2 minutes. Add 150 ml (¼ pint) water and the juice of the pared lemon. Bring to the boil, then lower the heat. Cover with a lid and cook gently for about 1-1½ hours or until the lamb is really tender.

5. Meanwhile finely chop the parsley. Finely grate the rind from the two remaining lemons.

6. Add the olives to the casserole with the grated lemon rind and half of the parsley. Season with salt and pepper. Add a little more water if the liquid has completely reduced, but not too much – it should be fairly thick. Cook for a further 10 minutes.

7. Peel and chop the red onion. Taste and adjust the flavour of the casserole, adding more lemon juice if necessary. Serve sprinkled with the remaining parsley, red onion and shredded lemon rind.

TECHNIQUE

Brown the meat in batches evenly all over, then return all the meat and onions to the casserole.

BEEF RENDANG

A deliciously rich beef dish from Indonesia. The meat is simmered in a spicy coconut milk until the liquid almost disappears – so it must be cooked in a wide casserole or saucepan or it will take forever to reduce. The dish tastes even better if made the day before and reheated. Serve with plenty of boiled rice or noodles.

SERVES 6

1 large onion, preferably red
6 garlic cloves
5 cm (2 inch) piece fresh root ginger
5 cm (2 inch) piece fresh or dried galangal
1 red pepper
4 dried hot chillies
10 ml (2 tsp) ground coriander
10 ml (2 tsp) ground cinnamon
5 ml (1 tsp) ground cloves
5 ml (1 tsp) turmeric
1.1 kg (2½ lb) stewing or braising beef
45 ml (3 tbsp) vegetable oil
1.7 litres (3 pints) coconut milk (see right)
1 lemon grass stalk, bruised
salt
finely shredded lime leaves, to garnish (optional)

PREPARATION TIME
15 minutes
COOKING TIME
About 2 hours
FREEZING
Suitable

955 CALS PER SERVING

1. Peel and quarter the onion. Peel the garlic, ginger and galangal. Halve the pepper, remove the core and seeds and roughly chop the flesh. Put all of these ingredients in a food processor or blender with the dried chillies, ground spices and 15 ml (1 tbsp) water. Process until smooth.

2. Remove any excess fat from the meat and discard. Cut the meat into large cubes, each about 6 cm (2½ inches).

3. Heat the oil in a large, wide flameproof casserole dish or a saucepan. Add the spice paste and cook over a medium heat for 3-5 minutes, stirring all the time.

4. Add the meat and cook for 2-3 minutes, stirring to coat in the spice mixture. (There's no need to brown the meat.)

5. Add the coconut milk and bring to the boil, stirring all the time. Add the lemon grass and about 5 ml (1 tsp) salt. Reduce the heat and simmer very gently, uncovered, for about 2 hours, stirring from time to time. The beef is ready when it is really tender and almost falling apart; the sauce should be well reduced and quite thick.

6. If the sauce is too thin, transfer the meat to a warmed serving dish, using a slotted spoon; keep warm. Bring the sauce to the boil and boil vigorously, stirring frequently, until sufficiently reduced. Pour over the meat. Check the seasoning before serving, garnished with shredded lime leaves, if available. Accompany with noodles or rice.

COCONUT MILK

Ideally use canned coconut milk as it has a good flavour and is easy to use. If unobtainable, you can use powdered coconut milk which is sold in sachets and needs reconstituting with water. Alternatively, use creamed coconut which is sold in blocks and also needs reconstituting. The latter can have a slightly cloying flavour; to counteract this add a little lime or lemon juice.

TECHNIQUE

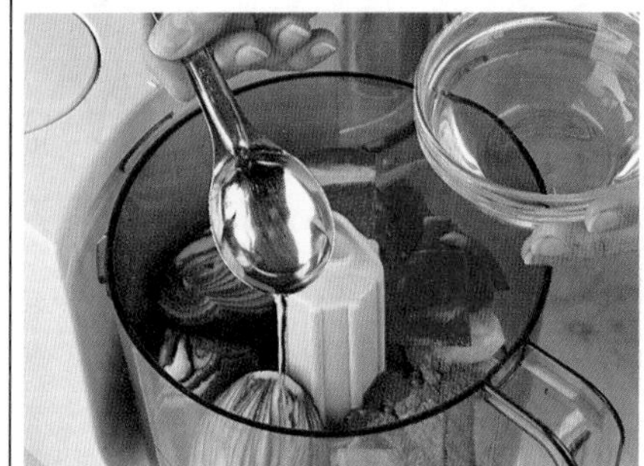

Put the red onion, garlic, ginger, galangal, red pepper, dried chillies, ground spices and 15 ml (1 tbsp) water in a food processor and work until smooth.

HOT AND SOUR BEEF SALAD

Chilli oil adds a distinctive flavour to this colourful salad. To make your own, pack fresh chillies into a clean glass jar or bottle. Pour on olive oil to cover and leave to infuse for at least 2 weeks before using. It improves with age, keeps almost indefinitely and is an attractive addition to the kitchen shelf!

SERVES 4-6

45 ml (3 tbsp) sesame seeds
salt and pepper
2-3 hot chillies
1-2 garlic cloves
2 large thick rump steaks, each about 300 g (10 oz)
juice of 3 limes
30 ml (2 tbsp) soy sauce
45 ml (3 tbsp) vegetable oil
8 spring onions
1 orange pepper
1 red pepper
1 cucumber
4-6 red shallots, or 1 red onion
1 lemon grass stalk, sliced (optional)
1 cos lettuce, head of Chinese leaves, or other salad leaves
handful of fresh mint leaves
handful of fresh coriander leaves
chilli oil, to taste

PREPARATION TIME
45 minutes, plus marinating
COOKING TIME
About 10 minutes
FREEZING
Not suitable

400-270 CALS PER SERVING

1. Toast the sesame seeds in a dry small heavy-based frying pan over a low heat until golden brown, shaking the pan constantly. Allow to cool, then crush with a pinch of salt, using a pestle and mortar.

2. Finely chop the chillies, removing the seeds if a milder flavour is preferred. Peel and slice the garlic. Put the steaks in a large shallow dish and sprinkle with the chillies, garlic and lime juice. Mix the soy sauce with 30 ml (2 tbsp) of the vegetable oil and drizzle over the meat. Leave to marinate in a cool place for at least 1 hour, or preferably overnight.

3. Meanwhile, trim the spring onions and shred very finely. Drop into a bowl of cold water. Quarter, core and deseed the peppers, then trim away the fibrous paler-coloured parts from the insides. Cut each pepper quarter into very thin shreds. Add to the bowl of water. Chill in the refrigerator.

4. Halve the cucumber lengthways and scoop out the seeds, using a teaspoon. Cut into thin strips, about 5 cm (2 inches) long. Cover and chill. Peel and finely slice the shallots or red onion.

5. Remove meat from marinade, reserving marinade; scrape off any garlic and chilli. Heat remaining oil in a large frying pan over a very high heat. Add 1 steak and press down to ensure that it browns evenly and quickly. Turn and repeat on the other side. Lower the heat slightly and cook for a further 2-4 minutes, depending on thickness and preference; ideally it should be rare-medium. Remove from the pan and cook the second steak in the same way. Cut into wafer-thin slices and place in a bowl.

6. Add the marinade and lemon grass to the pan. Simmer for 1 minute, then pour over the meat. Leave to cool.

7. Combine the lettuce, cucumber and half the drained shredded vegetables in a shallow serving dish. Toss with a little chilli oil and half of the toasted sesame seeds.

8. Add the shallots or red onion, mint and coriander to the beef and pile on to the salad. Top with the remaining vegetables and sesame seeds.

TECHNIQUE

Using a very sharp knife, halve each spring onion lengthways, then cut each piece into very fine shreds.

MEDITERRANEAN SALAD WITH HOT DRESSING

Serve this hearty main course salad with an interesting well flavoured bread – such as olive or tomato bread – and plenty of red wine. If you'd prefer to omit the feta cheese, replace it with a handful of assorted nuts – tossed in a little cumin and paprika and fried in the oil and butter used for cooking the croûtons.

SERVES 4-6

1 crisp cos lettuce
125 g (4 oz) French beans
225 g (8 oz) broad beans in their pods, or 125 g (4 oz) frozen broad beans
225 g (8 oz) feta cheese
6 artichoke hearts in oil (optional)
few sun-dried tomatoes (optional)
handful of fresh herbs, such as basil, oregano, parsley or chervil (optional)
salt and pepper

HOT DRESSING

1-2 dried red chillies
1 garlic clove, crushed
10 ml (2 tsp) balsamic or red wine vinegar
60 ml (4 tbsp) olive oil

CROÛTONS

3 thick slices of good bread
olive oil for shallow-frying
knob of butter

PREPARATION TIME
20 minutes
COOKING TIME
About 10 minutes
FREEZING
Not suitable

520-345 CALS PER SERVING

1. First make the dressing. Toast the chillies in a dry heavy-based frying pan over a moderate heat for 2 minutes, shaking the pan all the time so that they do not burn. Leave to cool, then crush. In a bowl, mix together the chilli(es), garlic and vinegar. Gradually add the oil, whisking all the time with a fork, to make a thick dressing. Season with salt and pepper to taste.

2. Trim the lettuce and separate into leaves. If the leaves aren't really crisp, immerse them in a bowl of chilled water while preparing the other ingredients.

3. Trim the French beans. Add to a saucepan containing a little boiling salted water and cook for 2 minutes. Drain, rinse with cold water, then drain thoroughly. Turn into a salad bowl and moisten with a little of the dressing.

4. If using fresh broad beans, remove from their pods. Cook in boiling salted water for 1 minute only, then refresh with cold water (as for French beans). Drain, skin if preferred, and mix with the French beans. If using frozen broad beans, place in a heatproof bowl, pour over sufficient boiling water to cover and leave until cool enough to handle. Drain, remove the skins if preferred, then add to the salad.

5. Drain and thoroughly dry the lettuce; tear into pieces. Toss with the beans.

6. To make the croûtons, cut the bread into large cubes. Heat the oil with the knob of butter in a frying pan. Add the bread cubes and fry until golden brown on all sides. Remove from the pan with a slotted spoon and drain on crumpled kitchen paper.

7. Break the feta cheese into large pieces. Halve the artichokes, if using. Chop the sun-dried tomatoes and herbs if using. Scatter the feta, artichokes, tomatoes, herbs and croûtons on top of the salad. Add the remaining dressing and season with salt and pepper. Toss lightly and serve immediately.

TECHNIQUE

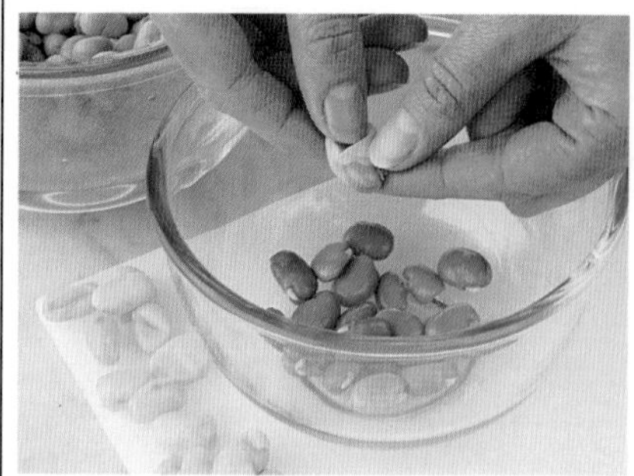

Once thawed, frozen broad beans can be easily skinned. Pinch one end of the skin to squeeze out the bean.

MINESTRONE WITH CHILLI PESTO

This classic Italian soup is served here with a fiery pesto sauce and freshly grated pecorino or Parmesan cheese. Serve as a main course with plenty of good bread, encouraging your guests to add a generous spoonful of the pesto to their soup.

SERVES 6-8

175 g (6 oz) dried haricot, cannellini or flageolet beans
salt and pepper
450 g (1 lb) potatoes
450 g (1 lb) carrots
2 large leeks
2.3 litres (4 pints) vegetable stock
1 dried red chilli
450 g (1 lb) courgettes
225 g (8 oz) French beans
425 g (15 oz) can chopped tomatoes
125 g (4 oz) pastini, or very small pasta shapes for soup
TO SERVE
Chilli Pesto (see page 9)
50 g (2 oz) pecorino or Parmesan cheese, freshly grated

PREPARATION TIME
20 minutes, plus overnight soaking
COOKING TIME
About 2-2½ hours
FREEZING
Not suitable

540-400 CALS PER SERVING

1. Put the dried beans in a bowl and pour on enough cold water to cover. Leave to soak overnight.

2. The next day, drain the beans and put them in a large saucepan with enough fresh cold water to cover. Bring to the boil and boil steadily for 10 minutes, then lower the heat and simmer for 1-1½ hours or until the beans are tender, adding salt towards the end of the cooking time. Drain thoroughly.

3. Peel and dice the potatoes and carrots. Trim the leeks and slice them fairly thinly. Pour the stock into a large saucepan and add the chilli. Bring to the boil, then add the beans, potatoes, carrots and leeks. Lower the heat, cover and simmer gently for 25 minutes or until the vegetables are really tender.

4. Trim and dice the courgettes. Trim and halve the French beans. Add to the soup with the tomatoes and pasta. Season with plenty of salt and pepper. Re-cover and simmer for a further 10 minutes or until the pasta is just cooked.

5. To serve, ladle the soup into warmed large soup plates. Hand the chilli pesto and grated pecorino or Parmesan cheese separately.

VARIATION

Use canned instead of dried beans. You will need two 425 g (15 oz) cans. Drain and rinse thoroughly under cold running water. Add to the soup towards the end of stage 4 to heat through.

TECHNIQUE

For the chilli pesto, process the toasted pine nuts, garlic, chillies and basil until finely chopped, before adding the olive oil, lemon juice and seasoning.

MIXED BEAN CHILLI

Serve this vegetarian version of the popular Mexican chilli with tortillas or rice. Ready-made tortillas are available from larger supermarkets and delicatessens, but you may prefer to make your own (see page 38). A generous dollop of soured cream and a sprinkling of Spanish Manchego cheese are ideal accompaniments.

SERVES 6

125 g (4 oz) dried red kidney beans
125 g (4 oz) dried black-eye beans
salt and pepper
1 red onion
3 garlic cloves
2-3 dried hot red chillies
700 g (1½ lb) mixed vegetables, such as carrots, potatoes, peppers, aubergines
60 ml (4 tbsp) olive oil
15 ml (1 tbsp) mild paprika
15 ml (1 tbsp) tomato purée
10 ml (2 tsp) cumin seeds
2 bay leaves
1 cinnamon stick
425 g (15 oz) can chopped tomatoes
15 ml (1 tbsp) lime or lemon juice
large handful of fresh coriander
TO SERVE
soured cream
grated Manchego or Cheddar cheese

PREPARATION TIME
20 minutes, plus soaking
COOKING TIME
About 2½-3 hours
FREEZING
Suitable

275 CALS PER SERVING

1. Put the dried beans in separate bowls and pour on enough cold water to cover. Leave to soak overnight.

2. The next day, drain the beans and put them in separate pans with enough fresh cold water to cover. Bring each to the boil and boil rapidly for 10 minutes, then lower the heat. Simmer until just tender: the red kidney beans will take 1-1½ hours; the black-eye beans 1½ hours. Add salt towards the end of the cooking time. Drain and rinse with cold water.

3. Peel and finely chop the onion. Crush the garlic. Crumble the chillies, removing the seeds if a milder flavour is preferred.

4. Prepare the vegetables, cutting them into fairly large chunks.

5. Heat half of the oil in a large saucepan or flameproof casserole. Add the onion, half of the garlic and half of the chillies. Cook, stirring, for about 5 minutes or until the onion is softened. Add the paprika, tomato purée and cumin seeds and cook, stirring, for 2 minutes. Add the bay leaves and cinnamon stick.

6. Add the beans and prepared vegetables, stirring to coat in the onion mixture. Cook for 2 minutes, then add the tomatoes and about 150 ml (¼ pint) water. Bring to the boil, lower the heat and simmer for about 45 minutes-1 hour until the vegetables are tender. If the mixture begins to stick, add a little extra water. About halfway through cooking, taste and add more chilli if necessary.

7. Meanwhile, whisk together the rest of the oil, lime or lemon juice and garlic. Roughly chop the remaining coriander and stir into the oil mixture. Leave to stand while the chilli is cooking.

8. When the chilli is cooked, stir in the coriander mixture. Check the seasoning if necessary. Serve with tortillas or rice, soured cream and grated cheese.

VARIATION

Use canned instead of dried beans. You will need two 425 g (15 oz) cans. Drain and rinse thoroughly under cold running water. Add about 15 minutes before the end of the cooking time.

TECHNIQUE

Whisk together the remaining olive oil, lime juice and crushed garlic, then stir in the coriander.

OKRA TAGINE

Tagine is named after the domed terracotta dish in which it is traditionally cooked. This is an attractive but rather cumbersome piece of equipment and not readily available in this country, so I suggest you use a casserole instead. If you come across preserved lemons in a Middle Eastern emporium, add a few to the tagine.

SERVES 4-6

2 onions
2.5 ml (½ tsp) saffron strands
30 ml (2 tbsp) olive oil
3 garlic cloves, crushed
5 ml (1 tsp) ground ginger
5 ml (1 tsp) turmeric
5 ml (1 tsp) caraway seeds
2.5 ml (½ tsp) ground cloves
10 ml (2 tsp) paprika
finely grated rind and juice of 1 lemon
300 ml (½ pint) vegetable stock
1 large head of fennel
handful of fresh coriander or parsley
3 fresh oregano sprigs
425 g (15 oz) can plum tomatoes
350 g (12 oz) okra
8 baby courgettes, about 225 g (8 oz)
handful of black olives
TO SERVE
harissa sauce (see note)

PREPARATION TIME
15 minutes
COOKING TIME
About 40 minutes
FREEZING
Not suitable

160-110 CALS PER SERVING

1. Peel and roughly chop the onions. Put the saffron in a small bowl, pour on 150 ml (¼ pint) warm water and leave to soak.

2. Meanwhile heat the oil in a large casserole dish, add the onions and garlic and sauté until softened. Add all the spices and cook, stirring constantly, for 2 minutes. Stir in the lemon rind and juice, the saffron with its soaking liquid, and the stock. Slowly bring to the boil.

3. Meanwhile, trim the fennel and cut into 6 wedges. Roughly chop half of the herbs. Add the fennel and chopped herbs to the casserole and season liberally with salt and pepper. Lower the heat, cover and simmer gently for about 15 minutes or until the fennel is softened.

4. Meanwhile drain the tomatoes, being careful not to break them up. Trim the stalk ends of the okra if necessary, being careful not to cut right through into the pod itself. Halve the baby courgettes lengthwise.

5. Add the tomatoes, okra and baby courgettes to the casserole. Simmer gently for 10-15 minutes until the okra and courgettes are cooked. Check the seasoning.

6. Add the remaining herbs and the olives. Serve immediately, with harissa sauce and plenty of bread, rice or couscous to mop up the juices.

NOTE: Harissa sauce is a hot pepper sauce sold in delicatessens and specialist food stores. It is a traditional accompaniment to many North African dishes.

VARIATIONS

- Add 175 g (6 oz) cooked or rinsed canned pulses, such as chick peas, with the fennel.
- Add 150 ml (¼ pint) thick yogurt with the tomatoes and okra, for a milder flavour.

TECHNIQUE

Pour 150 ml (¼ pint) warm water onto the saffron threads and leave to soak for about 10 minutes.

VEGETABLE PASANDA

Dry-frying whole spices like cumin and coriander releases maximum aroma and lends them a subtle smoky taste. The technique is used here to enhance the pasanda's rich, creamy flavour. To save time – if you must – add the spices straight from the jar in step 5, but make sure that you fry them sufficiently or they will taste 'raw'.

SERVES 6

75 g (3 oz) blanched almonds
10 ml (2 tsp) cumin seeds
5 ml (1 tsp) fennel seeds
10 ml (2 tsp) coriander seeds
5 cm (1 inch) piece fresh root ginger
2 garlic cloves
2 onions
6 cloves
8 black peppercorns
ghee or vegetable oil, for frying
300 ml (½ pint) double cream
350 g (12 oz) waxy potatoes
3 courgettes
1 medium aubergine
125 g (4 oz) green beans
225 g (8 oz) small cauliflower florets
450 g (1 lb) spinach leaves
salt
TO GARNISH
crisp-fried onions (page 48)
toasted shredded almonds

PREPARATION TIME
30 minutes
COOKING TIME
About 50 minutes
FREEZING
Not suitable

450 CALS PER SERVING

1. Put the almonds in a heavy-based frying pan and dry-fry over a gentle heat until just golden brown. Remove from the pan and leave to cool. Add the cumin, fennel and coriander seeds to the pan and dry-fry in the same way, shaking the pan all the time until the spices release their aroma. Leave to cool.

2. Peel the ginger and chop roughly. Peel the garlic. Peel and thinly slice the onions.

3. Tip the almonds into a food processor or blender and process until finely chopped. Add the ginger, garlic and 15 ml (1 tbsp) water. Work to a purée.

4. Crush the dry-fried spices with the cloves and black peppercorns, using a pestle and mortar.

5. Heat 30 ml (2 tbsp) ghee or oil in a large saucepan, add the onions and cook over a fairly high heat until tinged with brown. Add the almond mixture and cook for 2 minutes.

6. Add the crushed spices and cook for 2 minutes. Add the cream and 175 ml (6 fl oz) water. Bring slowly to the boil, then lower the heat and simmer very gently for 10 minutes.

7. Meanwhile, peel the potatoes and cut into chunks. Cut the courgettes and aubergine into chunks. Heat a little ghee or oil in a frying pan and fry these vegetables in batches over a high heat until thoroughly browned on all sides. Drain on crumpled kitchen paper.

7. Add the fried vegetables to the sauce with the beans and cauliflower. Simmer gently for 20 minutes or until the vegetables are tender; if the mixture becomes too dry, add a little extra water.

8. Meanwhile, trim and roughly tear the spinach leaves. Add to the pan and simmer for 1-2 minutes until just wilted. Add salt to taste. Serve garnished with crisp-fried onions and toasted almonds.

NOTE: It isn't essential to fry the potatoes, courgettes and aubergines. You can stir them straight into the sauce once it has simmered for 10 minutes, but they will take longer to cook.

TECHNIQUE

Dry-fry the almonds in a heavy-based frying pan over a gentle heat until just golden brown.

CRISPY NOODLES WITH VEGETABLES

Crisp deep-fried transparent noodles are tossed with stir-fried vegetables and topped with coriander omelette shreds. If preferred, flavour the omelette with 15 ml (1 tbsp) soy sauce instead of coriander.

SERVES 4

125 g (4 oz) thin, transparent rice noodles or rice sticks
vegetable oil, for deep-frying
2.5 cm (1 inch) piece fresh root ginger
175 g (6 oz) shiitake or button mushrooms
few Chinese leaves
1 red chilli
15 ml (1 tbsp) peanut or vegetable oil
125 g (4 oz) mangetouts
75 g (3 oz) beansprouts
30 ml (2 tbsp) soy sauce
30 ml (2 tbsp) dry sherry
5 ml (1 tsp) sugar
CORIANDER OMELETTE
2 eggs
30 ml (2 tbsp) milk
45 ml (3 tbsp) chopped fresh coriander
salt and pepper
a little vegetable oil or butter, for frying

PREPARATION TIME
20 minutes
COOKING TIME
About 10 minutes
FREEZING
Not suitable

390 CALS PER SERVING

1. To make the omelette, put the eggs, milk, coriander and seasoning in a jug and whisk together, using a fork.

2. Heat a little oil or butter in an omelette pan or small frying pan. Pour in the egg mixture and cook over a high heat until it begins to set. As it sets around the edge, use a palette knife to pull the set mixture towards the middle, letting the uncooked mixture run underneath. Cook until the egg is set all over.

3. Turn the omelette out onto a sheet of non-stick baking parchment and leave to cool. When cool, roll up and cut into thin slices.

4. Break the noodles into lengths, about 7.5 cm (3 inches) long. Heat the oil in a deep-fat fryer to 175°C (345°F). Test the temperature by dropping in a cube of bread – it should sizzle and become golden brown in 1 minute. Cook the noodles in batches. Deep-fry a small handful at a time for about 30 seconds until they swell and puff up. Remove from the pan with a slotted spoon and drain on crumpled kitchen paper. Don't cook too many at a time as they expand on cooking.

5. Peel and shred the ginger. Thickly slice the mushrooms. Coarsely shred the Chinese leaves. Slice the chilli, removing the seeds if a milder flavour is preferred.

6. Heat the peanut oil in a wok. Add the mushrooms and ginger and stir-fry over a high heat for 2 minutes. Add the chilli, mangetouts, beansprouts and shredded leaves and stir-fry for 1 minute. Add the soy sauce, sherry and sugar and cook for 1 minute to heat through. Add the noodles to the pan and toss to mix, being careful not to crush them. (Don't worry if they won't mix properly.)

7. Turn the vegetables and noodles into a warmed serving bowl and top with the omelette shreds. Serve immediately.

VARIATIONS

Stir-fry 50 g (2 oz) cashew nuts or almonds with the vegetables.

TECHNIQUE

When cold roll up the omelette, like a Swiss roll, and cut into thin slices.

COCONUT AND VEGETABLE SALAD

If you come across "yard-long" beans in an Oriental food store, buy some for this salad – it's the perfect way to show them off! As the name implies, they are very long beans. They may taste just like ordinary green beans but they certainly look extraordinary!

SERVES 4-6

2 large carrots
1 cucumber
6 spring onions
125 g (4 oz) yard-long beans or green beans
handful of baby spinach, or Chinese leaves or greens, such as pak choi
75 g (3 oz) beansprouts
handful of fresh coriander leaves (optional)
COCONUT DRESSING
1 garlic clove
15 ml (1 tbsp) vegetable oil
10 ml (2 tsp) curry paste
30 ml (2 tbsp) crunchy peanut butter
5 ml (1 tsp) chilli powder, or to taste
200 ml (7 fl oz) canned coconut milk
15 ml (1 tbsp) lime or lemon juice
15 ml (1 tbsp) soy sauce

PREPARATION TIME
10 minutes
COOKING TIME
About 15 minutes
FREEZING
Not suitable

200-130 CALS PER SERVING

1. Peel the carrots and cut into wafer-thin slices or fine matchstick strips. Cut the cucumber in half lengthways and scoop out the seeds, then cut into thin matchstick strips. Trim the spring onions and cut into thin strips. Trim the beans. If using yard-long beans either leave them whole or cut into more manageable lengths if preferred.

2. Bring a pan of salted water to the boil. Add the beans and blanch for 2 minutes, then rinse with cold water and drain thoroughly.

3. Trim the spinach or Chinese leaves. Cut or tear larger leaves into manageable pieces; if using baby spinach leave whole.

4. To make the dressing, peel and crush the garlic. Heat the oil in a small pan, add the garlic and cook for 1-2 minutes until softened. Add the curry paste, peanut butter and chilli powder. Cook for 1 minute, stirring all the time.

5. Stir in the coconut milk. Bring to the boil, then lower the heat and simmer gently for 10 minutes, stirring occasionally. Add the lime or lemon juice and soy sauce and mix thoroughly. Leave the dressing to cool for about 5 minutes or until it is just tepid.

6. Mix together all the salad ingredients in a serving bowl. Pour the dressing over the salad and serve immediately.

VARIATIONS

For a more substantial salad, add a few boiled new potatoes, and hard-boiled egg slices. Other vegetables, such as peppers, celery and mushrooms, could also be added.

TECHNIQUE

Using a teaspoon, scoop out the seeds from the cucumber halves and discard.

CARROT SALAD

This pretty salad is a good accompaniment to spicy meat and fish dishes. You could replace the orange slices with mango or papaya, or use blood oranges when they are in season. A few black olives scattered on top of the salad just before serving provide a striking contrast to the vivid shades of orange.

SERVES 4-6

450 g (1 lb) carrots
2 small thin-skinned oranges
few fresh chives, snipped
few small fresh mint leaves
DRESSING
1-2 garlic cloves
1 green chilli
1 red chilli
60 ml (4 tbsp) vegetable oil
5 ml (1 tsp) black mustard seeds
5 ml (1 tsp) cumin seeds
15 ml (1 tbsp) orange juice
15 ml (1 tbsp) lemon juice
salt and pepper
few drops of orange flower water

PREPARATION TIME
20 minutes
COOKING TIME
About 5 minutes
FREEZING
Not suitable

190-125 CALS PER SERVING

1. Grate the carrots, using the coarse side of a grater. (Do not use a food processor as it tends to make them very wet.) Pat dry with kitchen paper.

2. Peel the oranges, removing all the bitter white pith. Do this over a bowl to catch the juice (use for the dressing). Cut the oranges into very thin slices. Arrange the orange slices and carrots on a large serving plate and scatter with the chives and mint leaves.

3. To make the dressing, peel and thinly slice the garlic. Slice the chillies, removing the seeds for a milder flavour.

4. Heat half of the oil in a small pan, add the garlic and cook for 1-2 minutes until just golden brown. Add the mustard and cumin seeds and cook over a high heat for 1 minute, stirring all the time. Remove from the heat and add the remaining oil. Leave to cool.

5. Add the orange and lemon juices to the dressing with the chillies and salt and pepper to taste. Pour the dressing over the salad and turn the carrots and orange slices to ensure that they are evenly coated.

6. Leave the salad to stand at room temperature for at least 30 minutes to allow the flavours to develop. Sprinkle with a few drops of orange flower water just before serving, if liked.

NOTE: If using orange flower water, apply sparingly as the flavour can be overpowering.

VARIATIONS

Soak a handful of sultanas or raisins in a little orange juice until plump. Scatter over the salad before serving. For a more substantial salad, add a handful of cooked chick peas too.

TECHNIQUE

Peel the oranges as you would an apple, making sure you remove all the bitter white pith.

CHICK PEAS WITH GINGER AND TOMATO

This accompaniment is excellent served with baked potatoes or grilled sausages, or as part of an Indian meal. The flavour is improved if the dish is made the day before required and reheated. If you don't have the time for soaking and cooking dried chick peas, used canned ones instead – they work equally well (see variation).

SERVES 6

225 g (8 oz) dried chick peas
salt and pepper
5 cm (2 inch) piece fresh root ginger
1-2 garlic cloves
15 ml (1 tbsp) olive or vegetable oil
10 ml (2 tsp) garam masala
425 g (15 oz) can chopped tomatoes
2 spring onions
150 ml (¼ pint) thick yogurt or soured cream
5 ml (1 tsp) mild curry paste
30 ml (2 tbsp) chopped fresh mint
30 ml (2 tbsp) chopped fresh coriander (optional)
TO GARNISH
coriander sprigs
mint sprigs

PREPARATION TIME
5 minutes, plus overnight soaking
COOKING TIME
1¾-2¼ hours
FREEZING
Not suitable

175 CALS PER SERVING

1. Put the chick peas in a large bowl and pour on enough cold water to cover. Leave to soak overnight.

2. The next day, drain the chick peas and put them in a large saucepan with enough fresh cold water to cover. Bring to the boil and boil steadily for 10 minutes, then lower the heat and simmer for about 1½-2 hours or until the chick peas are really tender, adding salt towards the end of the cooking time. Drain thoroughly.

3. Peel and finely chop the ginger and garlic. Heat the oil in the saucepan and add the ginger, garlic and garam masala. Sauté for 2 minutes, then add the tomatoes and chick peas and bring to the boil. Reduce the heat and simmer gently for 15 minutes.

4. Meanwhile, trim and finely chop the spring onions. Place in a bowl with the yogurt, curry paste, mint, and coriander if using. Mix thoroughly and season liberally with salt and pepper.

5. Turn the chick peas into a serving bowl and swirl in the yogurt mixture. Serve immediately, garnished with coriander and mint sprigs.

VARIATION

Replace the dried chick peas with two 425 g (15 oz) cans of chick peas. Drain and rinse thoroughly under cold running water. Add to the tomato mixture, in step 3.

TECHNIQUE

Mix the chopped spring onions with the yogurt, curry paste, mint and coriander.

GRILLED AUBERGINES

Baby aubergines are ideal for this recipe. If you are lucky enough to obtain some, allow one per person, otherwise an aubergine half each should be ample as an accompaniment. If you're really short of time you could omit the degorging, but it does draw out any bitter juices and reduces the amount of oil the aubergines absorb during cooking. For a more substantial dish, to serve as a light lunch or supper, top with slices of feta cheese and accompany with a tomato salad.

SERVES 4

2 medium aubergines
salt and pepper
2 garlic cloves
1 green chilli
15 ml (1 tbsp) chopped fresh rosemary
finely grated rind and juice of 1 lemon
45 ml (3 tbsp) chopped fresh parsley
olive oil, for basting

PREPARATION TIME
25 minutes
COOKING TIME
15-20 minutes
FREEZING
Not suitable

125 CALS PER SERVING

1. Trim the aubergines and cut in half lengthways. Deeply score the flesh in a criss-cross pattern, cutting almost but not right through to the skin. Sprinkle generously with salt and leave to degorge for 20 minutes.

2. Meanwhile, peel and finely chop the garlic. Chop the chilli, discarding the seeds if a milder flavour is preferred. Mix the chilli with the garlic, rosemary, lemon rind and parsley.

3. Drain the aubergines and rinse with cold water. Squeeze dry. Brush the scored sides with olive oil and place, cut-side uppermost, on the grill rack. Grill – not too close to the heat – for 10 minutes. Spread with the herb mixture and drizzle with a little more olive oil. Position the grill pan closer to the heat source and grill for a further 5-10 minutes or until the aubergines are tender, brushing with more oil occasionally.

4. Arrange on a serving platter and sprinkle with a little lemon juice and olive oil. Serve immediately, with grilled meat or fish.

NOTE: If the aubergines are quite plump, increase the initial cooking time to 15-20 minutes.

VARIATION

Replace the chilli and herb topping with a coriander pesto. Place a handful of coriander leaves in the food processor with 1 green chilli, 2 peeled garlic cloves and 60 ml (4 tbsp) oil. Work to a paste and season with salt and pepper to taste. Spread on the aubergines and grill as above.

TECHNIQUE

Brush the scored surfaces of the degorged aubergines with olive oil before grilling.

SPICED POTATOES

For this accompaniment, choose firm potatoes with a good flavour. Look out for Charlotte, La Ratte, Pink Fir Apple, or any other interesting varieties that appear in the shops throughout the year. If you're short of time you could steam or boil the potatoes instead of baking them, but I think that the extra cooking time is worth the heavenly contrast of crisp-baked skin and buttery juices!

SERVES 4

700 g (1½ lb) small or baby potatoes
coarse sea salt
3 garlic cloves
2 mild green chillies
30 ml (2 tbsp) coriander seeds
15 ml (1 tbsp) black peppercorns
about 45 ml (3 tbsp) olive oil
2 spring onions
50 g (2 oz) butter
large handful of watercress sprigs, to serve (optional)

PREPARATION TIME
10 minutes
COOKING TIME
About 40 minutes
FREEZING
Not suitable

330 CALS PER SERVING

1. Preheat the oven to 220°C (425°F) Mark 7. Wash and dry the potatoes. Place in a single layer in a roasting tin. Sprinkle with coarse salt and roast in the oven for about 40 minutes or until tender. If your potatoes are very small they may take less time.

2. Meanwhile, peel and finely chop the garlic. Slice the chillies, removing the seeds if a milder flavour is preferred. Coarsely crush the coriander seeds and peppercorns.

3. Heat the oil in a small saucepan, add the garlic and cook until just beginning to brown. Add the coriander seeds and peppercorns and cook for a further 1 minute. Add the chillies and turn off the heat. Leave to infuse while the potatoes are cooking.

4. Trim and finely slice the spring onions.

5. When the potatoes are cooked, add the spring onions and butter to the spice mixture in the pan and heat gently until the butter is just melted.

6. Pile the potatoes in a warmed serving dish. Pour over most of the spiced butter and toss together. Scatter a generous handful of watercress on top if desired, and pour over the remaining butter. Serve immediately.

TECHNIQUE

Coarsely crush the coriander seeds and peppercorns, using a pestle and mortar.

VEGETABLE PILAU

This versatile pilau can be served as an accompaniment to any curried dish. It also makes a good basis for a vegetarian meal if served with a pulse dish, such as Chick Peas With Ginger And Tomato, and plenty of natural yogurt. If serving with fish, a little grated lemon rind is a good addition.

SERVES 4-6

125 g (4 oz) button mushrooms
about 175 g (6 oz) cauliflower florets
2-3 shallots, or 1 large onion
30 ml (2 tbsp) ghee, olive or vegetable oil
1-2 garlic cloves, crushed
1 bay leaf
2.5 ml (½ tsp) turmeric
6 cloves
6 cardamoms
1 cinnamon stick, halved
1 dried red chilli
350 g (12 oz) white basmati rice
125 g (4 oz) peas (optional)
salt and pepper
25 g (1 oz) butter (optional)
handful of roughly chopped fresh coriander (optional)
finely grated rind of 1 lemon or lime
toasted flaked almonds or chopped fresh coconut, to garnish

PREPARATION TIME
10 minutes
COOKING TIME
About 20 minutes
FREEZING
Not suitable

475-315 CALS PER SERVING

1. Thickly slice the mushrooms and cauliflower. Peel and halve the shallots; peel and thickly slice the onion if using.

2. Heat the ghee or oil in a heavy-based saucepan. Add the shallots or onion and cook, stirring, for a few minutes until beginning to soften. Add the garlic, mushrooms and cauliflower and cook briefly, stirring over a high heat, until softened and just tinged with brown.

3. Add the bay leaf and spices, and cook for 1-2 minutes, stirring all the time.

4. Add the rice, 600 ml (1 pint) water, the peas and plenty of salt. Bring quickly to the boil, then lower the heat, cover with a lid and simmer gently for about 10-15 minutes or until the rice is tender and the water absorbed. Add the butter and coriander if using, and the lemon or lime rind. Season with pepper. Re-cover and leave to stand for 5 minutes before serving.

5. Serve garnished with toasted flaked almonds or chopped fresh coconut.

VARIATIONS

Almost any vegetables can be used instead of – or as well as – the peas, mushrooms and cauliflower. Green beans, carrots, okra and courgettes are particularly suitable.

TECHNIQUE

Add the bay leaf and spices to the vegetables and cook, stirring, for 1-2 minutes.

Special ingredients, including spices, spice pastes and Thai ingredients, can be obtained by mail order from THE CURRY DIRECTORY, PO Box 7, Liss, Hants GU33 7YS; Tel 0730-894949